To Jo
Life is what you make it; have a good one.
Cecil Thompson
author 6-8-91
God Bless

*The Afro-American
Quest for Freedom*

The Afro-American Quest for Freedom

Black America's Quest for Peace

Cecil Thompson, Sr.

VANTAGE PRESS
New York • Los Angeles

FIRST EDITION

All rights reserved, including the right of
reproduction in whole or in part in any form.

Copyright © 1991 by Cecil Thompson, Sr.

Published by Vantage Press, Inc.
516 West 34th Street, New York, New York 10001

Manufactured in the United States of America
ISBN: 0-533-08730-9

Library of Congress Catalog Card No.: 89-90376

1 2 3 4 5 6 7 8 9 0

To the future black Americans
and coalition of Americans in general

Afro-American Pilgrim

This is my country, the only I know.
This is my country. Where else shall I go?
I have been here since American history began,
Fought in the wars to defend this land.

I have been lynched, downtrodden, and scorned,
Oft made to wish that I'd never been born.

Then one day I was able to see
That someone else was beholding me.

Someone who cared very much for me
Picked me up and set me free.

He freed me from prejudice, animosity, and hate,
Filled me with love and assured me my fate.

He promised me a home up in heaven above
If I overcome and continue in His love.

I'm glad I have accepted that Holy plight,
Where truth is the shadow of God, who is light.
—Cecil Thompson, Sr.

Contents

Foreword xi
Preface xiii
Introduction xvii

I. The Conflict 1
II. Activism 14
III. Truth Marches On 29
IV. A One-Thousand-Day Chronicle of John F. Kennedy 35
V. The Historical Wake 46
VI. The Aftermath 49
VII. No Alternative to Nonviolence 52
VIII. American History Complete and Unabridged 59
IX. The Revolution 71
X. Church and State 83
XI. The Moral Chagrin of the Churches 87
XII. Facing Facts 95
XIII. The Positive Black Catalyst in Washington 97
XIV. The Black Freedom Struggle 101
XV. Racist Proliferation 108
XVI. The Question of Race 117
XVII. The Classic March for Freedom 123
XVIII. Social Change 130
XIX. Aspiration to Black Unity 135
XX. The Presidency 145
XXI. What Does Jesse (Afro-America) Jackson Want? 160

Foreword

Cecil Thompson, the author of *The Afro-American Quest for Freedom*, is a product of the ghetto of the nation's capital city. He was an amateur boxer who was sparring partner with the late Eugene Smith when he became nationally known. Thompson also trained with Holly Mims and Stone Wall Jackson at Billy Edwards' Gym in Northeast Washington, under the watchful eyes of Joe Franklin and Bobby Brown. This year Thompson led his son, Cecil Thompson, Jr., to the Eastern Regent Championship of the U.S.A. Amateur Boxing Federation in Caesar's Palace in New Jersey. At this writing, Cecil Jr. is heading for the National Competition at Colorado Springs in quest of the Olympic games.

Cecil Thompson, Sr., attended school with Walter Fauntroy but dropped out of the 1951 graduating class to join the U.S. Marine Corps. After returning from the Marines, he finished his high school education with Roosevelt High School evening classes and attended the Modern School of Music. There he learned to play the bass fiddle, which enabled him to travel across the country with Buddy Loew's band, after having played a standing engagement with the Spa Night Club, once called the Off Beat Club, which during the Second World War was a famous landmark of black entertainment. Cecil Thompson, Sr., is a tour guide who speaks Spanish, French, and Italian fluently. (He is self-taught). He has travelled to London, Rome, Beirut, Lebanon, Syria, Jordan, and Tel Aviv, Israel, as a minister. He pastored the Craig Memorial Community Church and Miracle Gospel Mission for a total of ten years.

Mr. Thompson has received the 1988 Golden Poets Award from the World of Poetry in Anaheim, California. On September

2, 1989, the World Poetry Convention took place at the Washington Hilton Hotel, where again he received the Golden Poets Adward, with almost four thousand poets from around the world in attendance. Thompson is listed in the Marquis *Who's Who*, located at 200 East Ohio St. Chicago, Ill. 60611. He also has poetry in the National Library of Poetry in the Library of Congress.

In *The Afro-American Quest for Freedom* Mr. Thompson has focused on the repercussions of segregation in the United States and goes beyond the periphery of social stratification and its injustices to implement the Holy Bible to impinge upon anything contrary to righteousness.

In 1958, he met and married Ann Fitzgerald, who has served as the power behind the throne, but they both agree that the family that prays together stays together. Together they have raised a family of seven children, three girls and four boys, in a time when the gap between black and male and female is widening and the beleaguered black youths are striving to survive, apparently for lack of a unique, essential support system: The Family.

Preface

Life, with all of its failures, its heartaches and accomplishments, has been described by one writer of the Scripture as a vapor that appears for a little while then vanishes away. Though we live as if life, as we know it now, were eternal, we set our goals in life, and through blood, sweat, and tears we work hard to achieve them. I believe that William Shakespeare best desribed mankind when saying: "All the world's a stage." We make our entrances upon this colossal stage; we act out our roles and make our exits as the human drama goes on.

Alexander died in 323 B.C., before he had time to accomplish his plans for world unity. He had conquered most of the then-known world and created a world state. Many historians recognize that his central problem, the same as today, was, How can the people of the world live together in peace? Centuries later our Lord exploited the idea and made it palpable to millions yet unborn. Napoleon Bonaparte said, after having analyzed the failures of the empires of Julius Caesar, Alexander the Great, and his own: "Jesus Christ was no mere man; our empires built upon force, greed and hate are all gone but till this day, there are those who would lay down their lives for him," who was spoken of by the prophet Isaiah as the Prince of Peace. Jesus, the humble Nazarene, seeking to change the hearts of men, graced the stage and built upon love and, at the age of thirty-three, laid down his life and left a record towering above that of the world's great men of every age. The empty tomb in Jerusalem where once he lay is the only one with its claim in all the world. His disciples, who hid behind barred doors on the Sabbath morning of the

Resurrection, were, in a matter of weeks, changed from ignorant fishermen to fiery evangelists, orators, and heroes.

With the election of Jimmy Carter, there was an eruption of born-again believers in Congress. The public interest in evangelical Christianity was indicated by a 1976 Gallup Poll, which estimated that 50 million of the voting-age population had had a born-again experience. Shifting social pressures have pushed groups like the Moral Majority into prominence, and other less visible forces have arisen in and around the Senate. Sen. Roger Jepsen, Dr. Richard Halverson, and senators William Armstrong, Mark Hatfield, Strom Thurmond, and Lowell Weicker, Jr., are only a few of the Christians who made an impact on the secular world. Presidential candidate Jesse Jackson (of the Martin Luther King, Jr., constituency) did exploits in giving to the world the same message: "Righteousness exalteth a nation; but sin is a reproach to any people."

America must return to God, and exercised faith in the word of God must become, indeed, the power and the glory of our nation. Both black and white America must heed the admonition of God's word: "If my people who are called by my name will humble themselves and pray, seek my face, and turn from their wicked ways; then will I hear from Heaven, and will forgive their sin, and will heal their land."

Evil can prosper only as long as good is withheld; good withheld is a twin brother to evil exercised. The black man has been written out of American history and has not been given credit for many major accomplishments that helped to make our nation the greatest on the face of the earth. Notwithstanding, the black man has more reason to pursue the light than any nationality in this country because he has come the longest distance and has paid the greatest price to have liberty and justice and truth forever as a people. Perhaps the black man, in spite of oppression and exploitation, is, nevertheless, in an ideal spot to lead a spiritual crusade. But he must forgive in a true demonstration of Christian love. The white man must swallow his pride and seek forgiveness for racist attitudes of the past that have brought the current crises to our doorstep. Not to do so would be like a man lost in a cave who sees the light then deliberately goes the other way. A blind man, void of his sense, stumbling and groping in darkness, would be more to apt to find freedom than a man who denies the existence of the ball and chain by which he is hampered.

Introduction

In the midst of the crises of life, there is but one answer to every need, and it is Christ who is the author and finisher of the Christian faith. II Cor. 5:17 states: "If any man be in Christ, he is a new creature; old things are passed away and behold all things are become new." When this happens average men become giants and begin to do exploits.

The dramatic history of our country is filled with the words of these men who spoke from the depths of their character words indicative of their faith. Patrick Henry in 1775 said, "Give me liberty or give me death!" George Washington in 1787 said, "Let us build up a standard to which the wise and honest can repair." Abraham Lincoln in 1863 said, "That Government of the people, by the people, for the people, shall not perish from the earth." And they continue.

Emma Lazarus in 1886 said, "Give me your tired and your poor . . . I lift my lamp beside the golden door." Susan B. Anthony said, "Failure is impossible." Woodrow Wilson said, "The world must be made safe for democracy." Calvin Coolidge, a man who rarely wasted words, said in 1919, "There is no right to strike against the public safety, by anybody, anywhere, anytime." Franklin D. Roosevelt in 1933 said, "The only thing we have to fear is fear itself." William Allen White in 1940 said, "Liberty is the only thing you cannot have unless you are willing to give it to others." Dwight D. Eisenhower in 1953 said, "A people that values its privileges above its principles soon loses both . . ." John F. Kennedy in 1960 said, "And so, my fellow Americans. . ., ask not what your country can do for you; ask what you can do for your country. . ." and on human rights ". . .I believe in an America where religious intolerance will someday end. . .where every man has the same right to attend or not to attend the church of his choice. . .where there is no Catholic vote. . .and where Catholics, Protestants, and Jews. . .will refrain from those attitudes of disdain and division which have so often marred their works in the past, and promote instead the American ideal of brotherhood."

These words are from a few of the many thousands of truly great Americans; spoken in times of trials and circumstances which produced the causes, they could only be attributed to a people having a knowledge and awareness of an all-wise, all-just, and loving Father of all mankind.

Jesus said, "I am the way, the truth and the life." And in these times of political change, social revolution, drug abuse, race problems, sexual freedom, and the advent of the space age, these are the modern-day crises that must be dealt with. The great need of the hour is for man to find the right way, to know the truth and to have life. In the midst of the world's crises, Jesus is standing at the crossroads offering—to every individual and nation—to become their spiritual compass by day and their star by night, and the only way is truth, life, and perspective!

When we look at the achievements of Martin Luther King, Jr., George Washington Carver, Charles Drew, Bessie Smith, Jackie Robinson, Crispus Attucks, Laurence C. Jones, Benjamin Banneker, Richard Henry Boyd, Phyllis Wheatley, Mary McLeod Bethune, and Ethel Waters, who for many years were written out of American history because they were black while murderers, thieves, and rapists rated the headlines as stereotypes of the Afro-American people, it becomes a difficult task for us to lift up our voices with the status quo and sing with clarion sound, ". . . America! America! God shed His grace on thee and crowned thy good with brotherhood from sea to shining sea."

Educator Ernest O'Melby says that "No generation of Americans has talked so much about freedom as the present generation and none has shown so great a readiness to abandon it." When we sort it all out to determine just what "American freedom" is and what it isn't, we find that the word is kicked around like a football or like football players who have forgotten the location of the goal post. We play with it for all sorts of purposes, good and bad. Freedom is not something handed down from generation to generation, like the family silver or the old cuckoo clock; it is something that has to be won by each succeeding generation. Freedom is not a trophy cup won for us by our dead ancestors; it is a continuing process of which we are a vital part. Freedom is not the right to get anything we want, no matter how. ("Your freedom ends where my nose begins.")

Freedom is more of a headache than an heirloom—always a responsibility and never a license. When a youngster was asked to describe the famous picture *The Spirit of '76,* he said, "Well, in it there's one man with a fife and another with a drum and another with a headache."

Freedom is above all not an economic or nationalistic paradise. "It is a religious discovery," says Dale Evans Rogers, author of *Let Freedom Ring.*

*The Afro-American
Quest for Freedom*

Chapter I
The Conflict

On April 4, 1968, Dr. Martin Luther King, Jr., was cut down by an assassin's bullet. The tragedy took place at the Lorraine Hotel in Memphis, Tennessee, as Dr. King was standing on the balcony. When the news hit the airwaves and the papers gave details of the senseless murder, bedlam broke out on the streets of many of our cities all over the nation. Especially hard hit was Washington, D.C. The great freedom fighter had had a premonition while in Tennessee during an eight-day strike by the garbagemen. The mayor of Memphis, Henry Loeb, and city officials had refused to deal with black men who, at the time, worked under conditions inferior to those of their peers. The press never bothered to explain the facts of the incident that triggered King's assassination. The *Memphis Press,* police, and city officials had treated him as a troublemaker who should be eliminated.

In the wake of Dr. King's death, here in the nation's capital cars were overturned, Molotov cocktails with a burst of flames set fire to thousands of business establishments, and this continued far into the night. The blazing fires gave the city the appearance of an occupied war zone, as many of these fires roared out of control. Stampeding crowds were running and screaming as the sound of broken glass and other debris zoomed through the air. The stifling black smoke had created an ideal atmosphere for the looters and rioters who were busy in every part of town, sacking and burning at such a terrific pace that in most cases the police were powerless to quell the frenzied mobs on rampage. People scurried to and fro carrying stolen goods, while others spat out obscenities.

In the confusion and unrest, firemen and rescue squads with sirens blasting wound their way from place to place trying to put out fires or to be of some help. Wave after wave of stampeding crowds cleaned out liquor stores, which were prime targets. Many drank as they gave vent to their emotions, pulling whites from their cars and beating them brutally. At least one was pronounced dead on arrival at a nearby hospital in Virginia from such a severe beating.

Still shocked and dazed from the events of the day, I sat in my taxicab on the corner of Fourteenth and Harvard streets, N.W. My cab was being blocked by people who were walking in the streets to avoid fires, overturned trash cans, and other hazardous objects on the sidewalks, while I moved along at a snail's pace trying to pass them so I could proceed in the direction of home. At that time I lived in Anacostia, not far from the Fredrick Douglass home. Suddenly a voice cried out, "Hey, brother! I'm going your way." I then stopped drifting and came to a complete stop, and in so doing I found that, like myself, this man, too, lived in the southeast section of Washington. As he climbed in, there stood an old lady on the driver's side of the car who was begging to be taken also. I agreed and she got into the seat behind me, followed by a younger woman who appeared out of nowhere. I roared away from the curb, heading in the direction of Anacostia. As we drove a distance that seemed an eternity, we saw people carrying new clothes, food, and other stolen goods; one man even struggled with a floor-model TV set, trying to make it fit into a sports car.

As I drove, I thought to myself that in all of my years in Washington, D.C., I had never witnessed the things I was seeing then on the night Martin Luther King, Jr. was assassinated.

I was born and reared in Washington, D.C., watched the

changes being made, and also watched the city grow from a seemingly small town into the cosmopolitan world city that it is today. Nineteen hundred and thirty was the year of my birth. History records that it was the year that the Depression affected the lives of 4.5 million people. The State Department ordered a restriction placed on immigration, which prohibited almost any laborer from entering the United States. Again, in that eventful year the Bureau of Narcotics was formed as a unit of the U.S. Treasury Department. Sinclair Lewis was the first American to be awarded the Nobel Prize for literature. The population of the country at that time was 123 million.

Since the year 1935, I have seen a lot of changes in the city of Washington, D.C. The Montana Apartments, where we lived in the janitor's quarters, was one of the first homes to be replaced by an office building. The trolleycar that used to run up Connecticut Avenue, crossing M Street Northwest and out to Glen Echo, has been replaced by the underground Metrorail, and the bus now stops at that corner where the trolley once did. The little triangular park at M and Rhode Island Avenue, just across from Saint Matthew Catholic Church, seems to have shrunk to half the size it used to be. When I was five years of age, the little park contained the statue erected by the Hiberians of America in 1924. A ladies' auxiliary is the place where our family would go and sit at the end of the day, and some nights we would take a pitcher of lemonade. In my childhood imagination, the angel at each end of the statue would seem to come alive as we played about them. Many times since, I've felt that they were with me in an invisible form. Nevertheless, I remember the times we spent playing about the statues until the lemonade was gone and my father could be heard snoring on the park bench. Later he would signal to my brothers and me that it was time to turn in. Then there was twenty-five yards to go to reach home, where we would get ready for bed. Today most of the surrounding areas have changed, with the exception of Saint Matthew Church, the Jefferson Hotel at

Sixteenth and M streets, N.W., and the old Summer and Magruder school where I began my formal education. Quite a number of new buildings have been added; the Emerson and Orme Building, where Buicks were sold, has been replaced by the National Geographic Society. One block away, just in back of the old schoolhouse, is the B'nai Brith organization, one of the strongest Jewish powers in the world, located at Seventeenth and Rhode Island avenues, N.W. The funeral services for John F. Kennedy were held at Saint Matthew Catholic Church, which is now a tourist attraction as well as a place of worship.

Aside from my two brothers, I remember two other playmates from back in those days, whose family lived in our building and owned a bakery shop across the alley way, which faced on DeSales Street opposite the Mayflower Hotel. As children, sometimes we would play in the basement of the Montana Apartments, which my father would boast was one of the largest in the city.

Although my father had little formal education, he nevertheless had a fantastic talent for fixing things. He, like many people, drank occasionally and made mistakes, but he was proud of the fact that he was one of the founding members of the Greater New Hope Baptist Church in Washington, D.C. He taught me one thing that I never forgot—after he saw me put my hand up a little white girl's dress. It became a combination lesson: a premature one of the facts of life and the other one, which could be called "My Place in a Race-Conscious Society." It was the beginning of my education on racism. As the long green switch lashed across my back again, again, and again, I'll never forget hearing the words, "Never, never, never . . . as long as you're black, if you want to live and stay out of trouble, never let that happen again." Until I was a man, it never did. When I was old enough to start school, I learned that my playmates, Mary and Walter, went to another school and that all of the other kids at their school were of Caucasian descent. It got harder and harder for me to recite the flag salute, which I learned word for word before entering kindergarten. Soon after that I began to get suspicious and notice all of our white friends and the way they regarded us.

My father was a workaholic who got a kick out of fixing things. He was an electrician, carpenter, painter, and maintenance man all rolled up into one, which explains why someone thought it was a wise investment to have us live on the premises. But the stark reality of the double standard kept me on my guard lest I become disillusioned and fall victim to the American dream, which I thought was really not for me.

A few years later, we picked up and moved to Cincinnati, Ohio, during one of the worst floods in the history of that state. We quickly returned to Washington, D.C., and the ghetto life. Back in those days, aside from the then affluent Ledroit Park area, there were very few other dignified places for Negroes to live. The closest place to that area was an apartment up over the You and Me Restaurant, at the corner of Seventh and Florida avenues, N.W., with the entrance facing the old Griffith Stadium. When the Negro League came to town, we would find a way to get in to see all of the stars. Josh Gibson, one of the most famous of the time, would blast balls out of the park to land on Fifth Street three blocks away. Sachel Paige, then in his prime, would leave batters squinting to see the ball that thundered over the plate while the umpire called, "S-t-r-r-r-r-ike." Those were the good old days in Washington, and we were right in the heart of the Negro district, where anything could happen and usually did. One block below Florida Avenue was the Seventh and T Lounge, where the stars from the music world, who were appearing at the Howard Theatre, could always be found after the show, either there or in the Stage Door, Cozy Korner, the Nip-N-Sip, Cecilia's, the Cave, or at the other end of U Street at Alfred's Steakhouse. These were some of the places where black people congregated, laughing and joking as if there were no tomorrow.

Wandering back down memory lane is not all fun and adventure. There was also the sorrow and heartaches we experienced being black and growing up in the jungle of the nation's capital. That night of April 4, as we drove toward the southeast section, I tried very hard not to take on any more passengers or get blocked by fire apparatus, keeping mostly to the back streets when I could. Soon the eldest woman broke the silence, saying, "Mister, I'm so glad you stopped for me; I jes' wanna get home and off the street. Dis heah riotin' ain't gonna help nobody. Poh Martin was a good man, and he believed in peace. Why, dis ain't what he wanted."

At that, the younger woman, who had squeezed in beside her, said, "No, dis ain't what he wanted, but he got it just the same."

"Jes like all the rest, President Kennedy, Medgar Evers, Malcolm X, and everybody that tried to help this racist system change, they get killed."

"What else you gonna do when the man don' care nuthin' 'bout cha? Honey, we dun marched in, prayed in, and some dun got their teeth kicked in; it's too much, I tell you. I ain't dun no riotin' yet myself, but I can dig it, lady . . . You heah me, I can sho nuff dig it!"

Not another word was spoken for the rest of the trip. My first passenger and I looked at each other but said nothing. Soon each one reached his destination, paid, and got out and as I drove home, I reflected on all that had been said until I began asking myself, *What's the answer? Black people from all strata have voiced their opinions against slavery, lynching, and racist injustices visited upon ex-slaves; this had been done for many years, but to no avail.*

Black people—in their distress at having been torn from their loved ones, relatives, and friends; their language lost; survivors of the most perilous ocean voyages known to man; the most sought-after cargo in merchandizing history—reached these shores sick, emaciated, invalid, and confused with bitter memories of seeing brethren and fellow countrymen beaten to death, their women raped, and others jumping overboard to drown in the sea rather than continue a life of sorrow and servitude. The black people who did survive learned early how to worship God and seek the kingdom of God beyond the reach of the slavemaster's whip and the lynch mobs. Lynch law courts that executed nearly five thousand people in the United States from 1882 to 1962 were named after Charles Lynch, who took the law into his own hands during the American Revolution.

It was during this time that the old Negro spirituals we sing today were born. We worshiped the God of the only book we were allowed access to, maybe because it taught meekness and humility, servility, and turning the other cheek. In fact, few people—other than slaves—believed in the Bible to the point of practicing what it taught, most were so caught up in their lust for riches, that they became blind to the humanity of the slaves who were making them rich. Nevertheless, black people seized religion as a last resort, the same as a drowning man will reach for a straw. The Bible remains the hope of all mankind.

Almost four decades ago, in 1946, Paul Robeson went to the Lincoln Memorial with an irate protest while he was in Washington to see the president, who at that time was Harry S. Truman. Robeson's message was, "Stop the lynching; do something about it or Negroes will." The president said later that it sounded like a threat and added that he could not at that time do anything about it. Paul Robeson was one of the greatest Negro actors and bass baritones the world has ever known. He starred in the movie *The Emperor Jones* in 1933, and the production in which he played Othello in 1943 and 1944 had the longest single run on Broadway of any Shakespearean play on record. His other successes included roles in *The Hairy Ape, Black Boy,* and the motion picture, *Show Boat.* Robeson lost popularity when he became a champion of communism; the persecution that followed caused him to seek citizenship in another country. Robeson is one of the most unusual success stories in American history. He was too far ahead of the zeitgeist of his time to wait for the rest of Afro-America to gain sufficient strength to break the shackles of racism and be free. Someone has defined slavery as "unfreedom."

Looking back in history, we find that many thoughtful leaders of the American Revolution were troubled by the black man's status. They had gone too far in the name of freedom and the rights of man. If the believers in those rights were sincere, they could not honestly deny these rights to black people any more than to white. Yet that is precisely what slavery did. From the outset outstanding leaders themselves owned slaves. Gen. George Washington, for example, was a Virginia plantation owner; Comdr. Esek Hopkins, the first commander of the Continental Navy, was a former captain who had quelled a bloody slave uprising aboard his ship. There were a host of others who were by no means ready to do away with slavery or even to admit that it was wrong.

As early as 1776, when the Continental Congress asked Thomas Jefferson to write the Declaration of Independence for the colonies, the problem had begun to cause serious arguments. Today everyone remembers these stirring words from the Declaration: "We hold these truths to be self-evident, that all men are created equal, that they are endowed by their creator with certain unalienable rights, that among these are life, liberty, and the pursuit of Happiness . . . "

It is known, however, that Jefferson then went on to list the colonists' various grievances against George III of England. One of them was: "He has waged war against human nature itself, violating its most sacred rights of life and liberty, in the persons of a distant people who never offended him; captivating . . . or to incur miserable death of their transportation thither . . . " Most of the colonies had tried for a long time to enact laws that would stop or limit the slave trade. They had objected loudly when England had vetoed or ignored these laws, thus encouraging slavery. Yet the delegates of the Continental Congress from South Carolina and Georgia would not sign the draft of the Declaration, which blamed the king for the slave trade. They wanted nothing at all said about the buying and selling of slaves or about slavery, and the delegates from several other colonies agreed with them. As Jefferson himself wrote sometime later: "Our Northern brethren also, I believe, felt a little tender under these censures; for though their people have very few slaves themselves, yet they have been pretty considerable carriers themselves to others." The paragraph had to be taken out, therefore, and the whole troublesome slavery question was avoided.

In Paul Robeson's day, evasion of the issue had become systematic where the black man's rights were concerned. Thomas Jefferson was disappointed. Though a Virginian with a plantation and slaves of his own, he nevertheless was concerned over the evils of slavery. As he declared some years later, "Indeed, I tremble for my country when I reflect that God is just; that His justice cannot sleep forever." Later still toward the end of his life, he summed up the problem in a letter to a friend: "We have the wolf by the ears, and can neither hold him nor safely let him go. Justice is in one scale and self preservation is in the other."

It was true. The whole system of life in the South had depended on slavery for much too long. Other men who lived then realized, as Jefferson did, that slavery was wrong. Yet no one could see any practical way of putting an end to it.

So the answer to the unrest and the disorder of April 4, 1968, did not come from an eruption because of a single triggering or precipitating incident. Instead, it generated out of an increasingly disturbed social atmosphere, in which typically a series of tension-heightening incidents over the years had become linked in the minds of many of the black community with a reservoir of underlying grievances. Only a few years prior to the Martin Luther King, Jr., assassination, the black community had just witnessed the assassination of a symbol of living black manhood by the white power structure at the hands of black assassins. I'm speaking of Malcolm X, the gallant champion who did not turn from truth as he saw it to save his own life. In the mounting tension, the assassination of the black Baptist minister who advocated nonviolence was the breaking point. The single shot fired in Memphis, Tennessee, which severed the spine of Dr. King, also tore away the last bastion of patience remaining with black people all over the United States as temporary insanity swayed a bereaved people. Millions of dollars in merchandise and property were lost. The spirits of Nat Turner, Gabriel Prosser, and Denmark Vessey had revived and engulfed the crowds.

Mayor Walter Washington called on every available source of help that he could reach. Ministers, showmen, celebrities from all walks of life were being used to quell the angry mobs that had turned the city into a blazing inferno. Pres. Lyndon B. Johnson called in the National Guard, and only then, after, the curfew was imposed, was order restored. And again the country lost another man with a vision; when the smoke cleared and the last fire was extinguished, the big question was not Why? but, How long? How long would the people who professed to be a Christian nation before the eyes of the world keep silent while black people went on being exploited by the very same people who ran hither and yon trying to impress our black cousins who spoke another language.

Every true, born-again Christian's desire is that his friends will come to accept Christ as Lord. He does not want to cast them aside, as in James 2:16: "Depart in peace, be ye warmed and filled," thereby leaving them in the company of the demon of hate, presumptuously thinking that somehow their need will be met.

The fact that Martin Luther King, Jr., was a Baptist minister had little to do with the riot, except maybe because the vast majority of black people are Baptist and this might have added to the feeling of despair. After all, where black America is concerned, the church was one of the first places where black people were allowed to congregate freely. It was also the first organized assembly of black people in North America, and the pastor was automatically looked upon as the most influential person among the black congregation. It was the minister who took people's minds off the drudgery of life as second- and third-class citizens.

On Sunday, everybody is somebody in the Negro Baptist church. For a person who had worked hard all week, with little or no social functions to attend, it was always comforting to hear that our labor was not in vain in the Lord. And to hear the minister pray prayers that were sometimes repetitious: "When evening shadows do appear . . . when night has put on her purple garment . . . when we must go down to the riverside of Jordan, there is a friend called Jesus who will help you to cross over in a calm time, " was a comfort indeed.

So the assassination of the Baptist minister would kindle a spark of animosity. Nevertheless, the issue of human rights had taken priority over the religious aspect to the point that people had grown tired of the theory that promised "pie in the sky after you die." They had begun to hear any voice that advocated sociological change. Truth is the only known measure that can be used to evaluate both good and evil in the realm of earth, heaven, and hell in this time and space continuum; life is too short to go putting off for tomorrow what wisdom tells us should be done today.

We all know that religions are creeds and doctrines in the head and one does not become righteous because of a righteous mind. Religion does not mean righteousness (fear of God), as is stated in the Holy Scriptures. Religion represents concepts, ideologies, and traditions of man. While righteousness represents a moral responsibility to God, the two are not the same. Religion has been defined as the attitude of individuals in community to the powers that they conceive as having ultimate control over their destinies and interest.

We are the most religious country in the world because we have freedom of religion. And that freedom has caused experimentation with many new ideas. From the Pilgrim Fathers to this present day, Washington, more than any other city of its size in the nation, has more churches with different denominations than you will find anywhere else in the world. People in Washington hail from every corner of the globe, and they have brought their religions with them, but the only point where all agree is that we live in the twentieth century A.D. We accept the truth of Christ's birth and his death. The world has seen fit to date time from the calendar to show his birth and death and to attest to that fact of history. He lived on earth and he died. But religion based on that fact alone has no transforming power.

The Baptists when they first began in 1515 were called the Anabaptists. Then it is was agreed that Christians should be baptized in adult life after personally experiencing saving grace, as opposed to infantile baptism being the standard.

It was in the state of Rhode Island where the first modern principle of religious matters was allowed to prevail. This state was founded by the Baptist Roger Williams in 1639. He established the first Baptist church on American soil in the state of Rhode Island. That first church was divided between Calvinism and the broader appeal for all men to be saved. The question for saving grace caused them to be known as "particular or general Baptist."

The Civil War in the United States caused the church to be divided between the North and South, and it is today. Martin Luther King, Jr., realized that although he was a Baptist minister, religion was constantly changing and faith in one's God is a science of the heart. Today there is a popular advance in religion by comparision to the decline in Great Britain. Here in America, church services are popular and social life has replaced the gospel message in most congregations. There are innumerable youth groups and programs that center on worldly appeal rather than on the life of Christ.

A record of church affiliation from 1957 indicated 103,224,954 members. This is a gain of 3 million since the last count of members in 1955, which means that 62 percent of Americans are church members; a hundred years ago it was changed from 20 to 36 percent; the Catholics from 16 to 20 percent. The Methodist church leads the way as the largest single church in the United States, with 46,000 churches and over 9 million members.

The Southern Baptist Church has over 8 million members as opposed to 2 million members a generation ago. The largest Negro Baptist church is the National Baptist Convention church, with over 4 million members. The Episcopal and the Presbyterian churches (North) each have 2.5 million members. Some see this as indicative of a religious revival. Others see this as part of a complex pattern of motives, emotional, psychological, social, cultural groups that confounds easy analysis. Is it a return quest for other, more mundane, ends? One thing is certain: Americans of all faiths are attending churches or houses of worship as never before.

Chapter II
Activism

By Dr. King's actions it was evident that he had decided that out of necessity there must be a new venture, one built on truth and reality. For he was no longer content to preach the Gospel alone, but also to interpret the Gospel. In order to do this, he came down from his ivory tower to join the struggle in the streets. There in the streets is where the first American died for independence when black Crispus Attucks fell on King Street in Boston on March 5, 1770.

Thus, while the war for liberty was fought and won, slavery went on as before. Nevertheless, the years following the wars had brought important gains for many black people. In some parts of the North, so many slaves had earned their freedom by serving in the army that slavery was virtually wiped out. This happened in both Vermont and New Hampshire. There were far fewer slaves left in every northern state for the same reason. Equally encouraging was the fact that the war left strong antislavery feelings among Northern whites in general. In 1780, Pennsylvania became the first state to take steps to abolish slavery by law. By the year 1804 or shortly afterward, all other northern states had done likewise. Most of their new laws provided that the remaining slaves were to be freed only gradually, because they might compete for jobs with poor white workers if too many were freed at once. Some states made the process very gradual indeed. New York law, for example, granted freedom to a female slave only after twenty-five years of service to her master. A male slave had to serve for twenty-eight years. Taken as a whole, however, such laws spelled the end of slavery in the vast northern territory, which included all the lands lying north of the Ohio River and west of the Mississippi. This act had very little effect at the time. Most of the region was still wilderness, inhabited only by Indian tribes, which acknowledged no allegiance to any white man's government.

Moreover, the law was passed only on condition that all the territory south of the Ohio should remain open to slavery. In addition, all runaway slaves who fled into the Northwest Territory had to be returned to their masters if they were caught. Southern members of Congress insisted on these two provisions. In spite of them, the law meant that black men and women would be assured of freedom in the great future states of Ohio, Indiana, Illinois, Michigan, and Wisconsin.

There were other gains as time went by. Many white people realized that the former slaves would not find it easy to make their way in the world as free men. Schools to train them were set up. One of the first was the African Free School, founded by the New York Manumission Society in 1787. It opened with forty students. Soon there were similar schools in nearly every northern city.

Classes were often held for black children during the day and for men and women at night. When these freed people had been trained, they were given help in finding jobs. School officials frequently checked afterward to make sure that black workers were being treated fairly by their employers. Because they were usually segregated in white churches, black men and women soon founded congregations of their own in almost all faiths. Such groups became important agencies of self help for black people. Many outstanding leaders at the time, in fact, were black ministers. A few became so well known that they were asked to preach in white churches as well as black ones.

Various societies for the betterment of black people reached out in all directions. They went on urging state legislatures to pass more laws benefiting the black man—slave as well as free. They did their best to make sure that masters and employers obeyed the laws already in force. They worked tirelessly against everything connected with slavery and the slave trade. In fact, these societies were the founders of the abolitionist movement, which was destined to grow and become stronger in the years ahead.

The task they had set for themselves was difficult and often discouraged. The vast majority of white people everywhere still thought of black people as members of a lower race, who simply did not have the ability to be the white man's equal. This view was common even among the abolitionists themselves. Their efforts to help black men were due to kindness rather than to any true belief in black equality. Yet some black men and women succeeded in becoming shining examples to their own people and to whites alike.

Two of the most noted black men and women during this period were Phyllis Wheatley and Benjamin Banneker.

Phyllis Wheatley was born in Africa. She was still a small child when slave traders captured her, carried her across the sea, and sold her in Boston. Fortunately, she fell into the hands of a good master who saw that she received a good education equal to that of most white children of that time. The little girl quickly learned Latin and became acquainted with classical English literature. Taken to church with her master's own family, she became deeply religious. Soon her intelligence and charm made her a favorite of the entire white congregation.

Phyllis began to write poetry when she was still a girl in her teens. Gradually, her poetry began to attract widespread attention in the Boston area. Later she visited England, and there too people were charmed and amazed by her talent. Many years after her death, a collection of her poetry, published by abolitionist societies and titled *The Memories and Poems of Phyllis Wheatley,* was still being read and admired.

Benjamin Banneker's story was even more remarkable. Unlike Phyllis Wheatley, he was born free, though his father had been brought into Maryland as a slave. In school, young Banneker showed such cleverness at science and arithmetic that some of his teachers loaned him extra books and urged him to go on studying. Eventually, he grew up to be an astronomer and a mathematician whose works were honored by leading scientists in both this country and Europe. For several years he wrote and published one of America's first almanacs. He also learned to be an excellent surveyor.

Each time I take a tour group to the L'Enfant Plaza, where Banneker Circle is, in the southwest area of the U.S. capital, I am reminded that this was yet another black voice that spoke to the moral conscience of the nation over the racial issue of slavery. Benjamin Banneker was born near Ellicott Mills (now Ellicott City, Maryland).

Banneker's formal education was limited to attending a Quaker school near Joppa, Maryland. His mother, Mary, was the eldest daughter of Molly Welsh and an African prince named Bannsky, whom Molly had purchased and later married. So Benjamin Banneker was born free following the status of his mother, rather than that of his free-man father, Robert. Robert took his wife's name, which had been anglicized to Banneker.

Benjamin Banneker was a favorite of his grandmother, who taught him to read the Bible at her knee before he was of school age. He became an avid reader and a self-educated genius. Benjamin Banneker has an impressive list of accomplishments to his credit. He made the first American clock while he was still a youth, a wooden clock that struck the hour; he published one of the first and most successful almanacs in this country, containing tidal information and astronomical observations, including the successful predictions of the eclipses, and medical formulas. Benjamin Banneker greatly impressed Thomas Jefferson, who found Banneker's almanacs every bit as helpful as Benjamin Franklin's *Poor Richard's Almanac*.

In 1719 Banneker sent the manuscript of his new almanac to fellow scientist and admirer, secretary of state Thomas Jefferson. In sending his gift, Banneker took the opportunity to suggest that, if the secretary of state admired Banneker's work so much, he might also be interested in freeing black folks. What he reflected was in the language patterns of his era. "I freely and cheerfully acknowledge," said Banneker in his letter to Thomas Jefferson, "that I am of the African race and in that color which is natural to them of the deepest dye; and it is under the sense of the most profound gratitude of the supreme rule of the universe, that state of tyrannical thralldom, and in human captivity which too many of my brethren are doomed."

Banneker said to Jefferson he was making reference to the famous words that capitvate millions of tourists from all over the world who visit the Jefferson Memorial each year during the tourist season; they are the words of the Declaration of Independence. "We hold these truths to be self evident: that all men are created equal, that they are endowed by their creator with certain inalienable rights and that among these are life, liberty and the pursuit of happiness . . ." Banneker also reminded Jefferson that at the time he wrote these words he clearly saw into the injustice of the state of slavery and had just apprehensions of the horror of it conditions, stating that his abhorrence then was so excited that he publicly held forth this true and invaluable doctrine, which was worthy to be remembered in all succeeding ages. Banneker accused Jefferson in a surreptitious manner that tender feelings for himself had engaged him thus to declare, that Jefferson was then impressed with proper ideas of the great violations and the free possessions of those blessings to which he was entitled to by nature. But Banneker also reflected on the fact that although Jefferson was fully convinced of the benevolence of the Father of all mankind and his equal and impartial distribution of these rights and privileges that he had conferred upon him (Jefferson), he should at the same time himself be found guilty of that most criminal act, which he had professedly protested in others with respect to the slaves that he owned.

Needless to say, that secretary of state, Jefferson, was anything but condescending in his reply; he thanked Banneker sincerely for his letter and the almanac that it contained, calling it a letter of the nineteenth instant. The Library of Congress contains these letters and many more valuable documents revealing the greatness of this country.

It is evident from Jefferson's letters to Banneker that Jefferson held a high regard for him as a man of equal intelligence to his own. Even though Jefferson was the man who mastered all of the learning of his day, he had come to respect Banneker, whose only difference from his brethren was that he was free from the manacles of slavery and he was self-educated and thus was able to meet Thomas on a footing of equality. One of the greatest causes of bigotry, hatred, and fear in this country is the fear the white man harbors—that of being placed on a footing of equality with the black man. He feels that if this should happen he cannot win. Why else the fear of competing?

Also in Jefferson's letter was the racist ideology maintained by the white status quo: procrastination and tokenism. Usually, while we are learning the long, hard lesson that tomorrow is Satan's substitute for today, tokens are used to slowly but surely keep things as they were. Today we have constant reminders via television and radio commercials: "A mind is a terrible thing to waste. Support the Negro College Fund." And they go on ad infinitum. I am not one to put a premium on ignorance, but far too many times after becoming proficient in a trade or professional career, blacks are often confronted with other barriers that require far too much patience to go around. Here we reiterate the words of Rev. Jesse Jackson, who reminded the United States prior to his campaign in 1984 for the presidency, "I am somebody." And black Americans who are striving for mastery show by our persistence in well doing may well repeat the words, "I am somebody," and then go on to prove it by exploits with our education. As I have said before, "Black people, through toil and sweat, have helped to build this mighty nation. The years of free and cheap labor have gone without due compensation."

Banneker also learned to be an excellent surveyor. Banneker's prominence was recognized when he was asked to serve with a national commission to plan and survey the city of Washington, the new capital of the United States. Very few white men could match his records of success in so many different fields.

There were not many like Banneker and Phyllis Wheatley, of course. Few black men or women were lucky enough to be given the advantages and encouragement they received. On the contrary, the majority of free slaves had to overcome the serious handicaps of ignorance, humility, and unthinking obedience, which had been forced on them during years of bondage. All too often they found that freedom brought only hard work, disgust, disappointments, and bewildering new problems. Yet those final years of the 1700s were better than most black people had ever known in the past. Even in many parts of the South, the old black codes governing slavery no longer were strictly enforced.

On May 25, 1787, a convention met at Philadelphia, Pennsylvania, to draw up a constitution for the United States. Once more the old slavery question came up for argument. Men from the South still were determined that the slave trade, they insisted, must be allowed to continue. They were ready to agree that it was an evil thing perhaps, but a necessary evil.

The War of Independence had left many plantation owners worried about their supply of slaves. The British, as we have seen, had freed thousands of slaves and taken them out of the country. Many more had run away during the war. Most states, even Maryland and Virginia in the South, already had made the slave trade illegal. Considering these facts, said the delegates from South Carolina and Georgia, it would be unfair to stop the trade until they had had time to bring in the new slaves they needed.

At last, since neither North nor South would give in completely, a compromise was reached.

By its terms, the words *slaves, slavery,* and *Negro* did not appear anywhere in the final draft of the Constitution of the United States. Thus the issue was sidestepped once again, and slavery was neither approved nor disapproved. In return, northern delegates agreed that the federal government could do nothing to stop the slave trade for a period of at least twenty years.

This actually amounted to a pretty poor "compromise" from the northern point of view. By saying nothing, it accepted the existence of slavery; worse than that, it shamefully ignored the moral principles involved and belied the glowing words of the Declaration of Independence. In justice to the northern delegates, however, it is doubtful that any constitution could have been adopted without the compromise. The slavery interests simply were too powerful, too determined, and too firmly united.

Another argument arose over the number of men the states should elect to Congress. It was soon decided that they should each have two senators, while the number of members a state could send to the House of Representatives would depend on that state's population. The South claimed that slaves ought to be counted as well as white men. The northern delegates objected. Slaves were not permitted to vote, they pointed out. Slaves were not citizens at all. Indeed, the southern states' own laws gave slaves no human rights of any kind, so it made no sense to count them on the same basis as the whites. As Oliver Ellsworth of Connecticut put it: "Slavery in time will not be a speck in our country!"

Mr. Ellsworth undoubtedly meant well, and his opinion probably was shared by a good many others. But he was a very bad prophet. Slavery was not dying. Within a few years, it began to grow stronger and more widespread than ever.

Gradualism, the linchpin of segregation and slavery, working as a tranquilizing drug upon the United States, has never ceased to wreak havoc upon the greatest country on the face of this earth.

When the Constitution of the United States was drafted, mighty forces already were at work in both Europe and the United States. Hardly anyone realized it at the time, but those forces were about to bring far-reaching changes into the lives of everyone, white and black alike.

They had begun with the invention of the steam engine by a Scotsman named James Watt, in the year 1769. Watts's first engine was a crude affair, but soon improved models of new machines appeared. The machines, in turn, were able to do a wide variety of jobs that always had been done by men or by beasts of burden in the past. The machines did the work faster and more cheaply than ever before. Slowly at first, but steadily, too, goods began to be turned out by large factories instead of by craftsmen working in their own homes or small shops.

This movement, known as the Industrial Revolution, eventually created the world in which we live today. Among the earliest changes it brought to the United States was a new and valuable crop for the South: cotton. Planters had begun to grow a little cotton in the colonies long before the War of Independence. Most of it was made into cloth by small spinning wheels and looms that were made by hand. The work was usually done by the women of individual families, who used the cloth for their own needs. Raising cotton for sale did not become profitable until machines were developed in England to spin into thread and then to weave the thread into cloth on a larger scale. Even then, the crop had one great drawback that held the profit down. The soft cotton fibers in the pods, or bolls, clung to the seeds so tightly that picking them apart was a long, tedious task. The most skillful slave, working as hard as possible, could separate only about a pound of lint, as it was called, in a whole day's time. Thus it was next to impossible to prepare large quantities for market. The problem was only partly solved by the introduction of Sea Island cotton, a new variety in which the lint was somewhat easier to separate.

Then Eli Whitney, a young schoolteacher from New England, built the first mechanical cotton gin while visiting a Georgia plantation in 1793. His machine consisted of a roller studded with metal teeth that pulled the cotton lint through a wire screen but left the seeds behind. It worked so simply that a single slave, doing little more than turning a crank, was able to produce as much as fifty pounds of lint a day.

Plantation owners were quick to see the advantages of the Whitney machine. Presently, bigger and better gins driven by steam engines were built. These could turn out still more lint. Soon cotton production began to rise like magic.

Almost overnight—within a very few years, actually—cotton became the most important crop in the South.

Records still in existence show some of the enormous profits that were made. A South Carolina planter grew rich enough to retire in the three years from 1796 to 1798. He sold his plantation at a price most of his neighbors felt was far too high. Yet the man who bought it made every cent of the price back from the cotton he raised in the next two years. Another man, who planted cotton on three hundred acres, figured out the value of the crop according to the number of slaves who worked on it. Each slave, he discovered, had earned $509 for him. Considering that such a plantation might employ one hundred slaves or more often many times that number, the prospect of making large sums of money was excellent indeed.

Figures like these were not unusual, and they spoke of themselves. As it happened, cotton came along just when many plantation owners were beginning to complain of hard times. The profits from raising tobacco had been falling steadily for years. Some slave owners were feeling the pinch so badly that there was a rueful little joke among them. Instead of runaway slaves, they said, soon the country would be hearing about runaway masters.

Now all that was changed and large gangs of slaves became

more valuable than ever to their masters.

Cotton was well suited to the use of slave labor. In the mild southern climate, it grew all year round, so there were few slack seasons during which slaves failed to earn their keep. The plow and the hoe were the only tools used for cultivation. Picking the cotton under the hot sun was a tiresome form of drudgery, but it required no great physical strength. Old as well as young, women, and even little children could be put to work at it. Besides, cotton was a hardy crop. It was much more satisfactory in this respect than tobacco, which required both care and skill.

Unlike rice, which could be raised only in the warm, wet lowlands along the seacoast, cotton grew well in almost all kinds of southern soil. Best of all, from the plantation owners' point of view, the operators of textile mills in England, and later in the northern states too, were greedy for all the raw cotton they could get. No matter how much was raised, prices and profits remained high.

Wealth began to increase rapidly throughout the South. Planters built splendid large homes for themselves and their families. Their wives and daughters enjoyed costly gowns and bonnets from Paris. Their sons went to expensive schools or took long trips to Europe. In effect, these people became the rulers of a new American kingdom: the cotton kingdom, based on cheap slave labor.

Cotton was one of the factors that encouraged southern pioneer families to move into frontier regions to the west. Most of these people were small farmers; few of them owned slaves, and many never would. But among them were ambitious men who realized that cotton offered their best hope for success and prosperity in the future. They looked forward to settling on virgin land and becoming planters and slave owners as soon as possible.

Tennessee was admitted to the Union as a state in 1796. Some men there already had begun to raise small amounts of cotton. They shipped it to market in a long and roundabout way on flatboats that floated down the Cumberland and Mississippi rivers to New Orleans. Farther to the south and west other frontier territories also were attracting settlers. The soil and climate provided ideal land for growing cotton. The territories would become Mississippi and Alabama, two of the greatest cotton states of all.

The cotton kingdom was growing, and as it grew, its power in Congress steadily increased.

All of this meant new life for the slave trade. Cargoes of black men and women, fresh from Africa, were eargerly sought after by buyers in the seaports of Georgia and South Carolina. In addition, a slave trade grew up among the states themselves, despite the fact that most of them had laws forbidding it. Tobacco planters in Virginia and Maryland, finding themselves with more slaves than they could support, were only too happy to sell some of them to cotton planters in other states.

With money to be made, the laws were soon repealed, changed, or simply not enforced.

Increasing property brought a new attitude toward slavery itself. Southerners no longer were willing to admit that it was a "necessary evil" as many of them once had. Instead, they took to calling it a positive force for good. Several years later, when this feeling had become general in every southern state, a Virginia attorney named George Fitzhugh wrote a book defending it. Said he: "The negro slaves of the South are the happiest, and, in some sense, the first people of the world. The children and the aged and infirm work not at all and yet have all the comforts and necessities of life provided for them. They enjoy liberty, because they are oppressed neither by care nor labor." Perhaps some people honestly believed this nonsense. A great many others undoubtedly knew better but preferred to convince themselves that it was true. For every foreseeing man of the caliber of Thomas Jefferson there were hundreds more who refused to be concerned about slavery at all.

Similar points of view became general even in northern

abolitionist societies; alarmed and horrified by the spread of slavery, they continued their efforts to fight it, but a kind of hostile reaction had set in among other white people. The enthusiasm for liberty and the rights of man that had swept the country for a while was dying down. Much of it always had been more words than acting, to be sure; now even the words were forgotten. Many white people felt that black men already had received enough help and ought to shift for themselves. Resentment was growing among poor and unskilled white workers who claimed free black men were taking their jobs away.

Much of this was natural, no doubt. Nevertheless, it meant a severe setback for the black man's long, hard march toward true freedom and equality. For the thousands of slaves in southern cotton fields freedom had become a lost hope. This was the state of affairs when a new black hero arose to kindle that hope.

Word of him came across the sea from the West Indies, where slavery in America had first begun, and so the days rolled into weeks, weeks into months, and months into years. Slaves moved on in quest of freedom. Keeping pace with the spirit of truth, Dr. King, with his scholastic ability and knowledge, turned to confront the real enemy who insisted that black people remain second-class citizens. Dr. King, a devout student of Mahatma Gandhi, the progenitor of nonviolence and peaceful resistance, took a page from the book of Isaiah 1:18: "Come now, let us reason together." Dr. King, using dialogical reasoning, seized upon the case of Rosa Parks, the distinguished black lady who was riding on the bus in Alabama, seated in the white section of the bus and was asked to move. For some reason she did not. Perhaps God dispatched an angel from the halls of justice on high telling her that "the set time is come." (Psalms 102:13) For that reason, she decided that she would not move and thus attested to her right to ride where any other person might choose to ride.

The ensuing struggle following that ordeal was not confined to a question of black or white, but between the forces of good and evil, right and wrong. She was put off the bus and placed under arrest. Thirty or forty others heard about it and converged upon the scene at the jail where she was being held in protest of the unjust arrest. They too were jailed, but they found themselves bound together in a fellowship of common cause and devoted not only to it, but to one another. Hundreds of others heard about the action and came together in protest, and in the end almost a thousand people expressed their conviction, accepting suffering in order that justice might be done and the cause of God served.

This was the new congregation operating under a primitive theology, which Dr. King was to speak to, one unequal to the task of the traditional congregation. The question was, Would it be possible for the old congregation to offer itself to the new in such a way that the historic theology of the Christian church might be available to sustain the new movement, in order that it might find itself and its resources? The old congregation was so different, so wild, and so unrespectable to its new method of operating. This new ministry, namely reconciling man to man, truly brought together the congregation of God's people.

From the Alabama boycott to the Memphis strike, Dr. King was at the forefront of every battle in the name of nonviolent demonstrations. He will be revered in the hearts of the people. Americans and people the world over, both black and white, will praise him, not only because he was awarded the Nobel Peace Prize, but because he did what he felt was in accordance with the zeitgeist, whether or not it demanded his life.

The United States has suffered slavery, civil war, deep depression, and world wars on both sides of the globe. The dedication of great Americans throughout the history of this country has proven the strength of this Constitution. The Watergate fiasco only proved again that even the president of the United States is not indispensable when he trifles with the Constitution of this country. Civil rights demonstrations in adherence to the Constitution have brought changes in our system of government. John F. Kennedy and the Rev. Dr. Martin Luther King, Jr., were indispensable to civil rights and the struggles of the sixties. The assassinations that shocked the world should have taught us that we need not live up to the saying that "assassination in America is as endemic as apple pie." As a nation, the United States made grave mistakes, but there is no need to make them again. In spite of the fact that there are mountains to climb and much land to possess in the area of civil rights, we have been through certain phases and there is no need to go through them again. The United States began with the right spirit, by her faith in God. The founding fathers were using the same truths of which George Washington spoke: "Let us raise up a standard to which the wise and the honest can repair." Likewise, the nonviolent civil rights movement was a campaign against unjust laws or laws that were binding on a minority and not on the majority. It must be remembered that "righteousness exalteth a nation; but sin is a reproach to any people." (Proverbs 14:34).

One answer to racism lies in the urgently needed new history that will put the study of the past in the present and the future. Such a demand will give American history the proper perspective for the most constructive society ever in the United States of America. We are too prone to identify the American heritage as a Euro-American history and to forget that we are an Afro-American invention as well.

The Black American Brother

But don't call me Brother only because I'm black.
If you must call me Brother, lift the load from my back.
When you call me Brother, be sure you're sincere
And remember that in chains I was first brought here.
I'm often related to debauchery and sin
And much ostracized for the shape I'm left in.
From the manacles of slavery the process was slow
And my uphill climb filled with penury and woe.
When you judge me not by the color of my skin
Then call me Brother, and I'll be your friend.

Chapter III
Truth Marches On

Countee Cullen, a famous black poet who lived from 1903 until 1946, praised black kings and men of power, saying of Henry Christophe, Dessalines, and Toussaint-Louverture the following:

> Those men were kings, albeit they were black
> Christophe and Dessalines and L'ouverture
> Their majesty made me turn my back
> Upon a plan I once shaped to endure.

The tribal elders are the wise old men whose job it is to remember the past from the remotest antiquity and to pass the knowledge on to the young that their ancestors were not savages squatting along the banks of the Congo, the Niger River, and the Blue Nile. They were explorers, children not of the darkness, but of the sun, and they wandered without let or hindrance to places where no man has ever been before. One could not look them in the eyes because their faces were so bright that it hurt one's own eyes to look at them. The whole of Negro history, from ancient Africa to present, reveals an African civilization far beyond the Darkest Africa that was only in the minds of those who went to exploit and enslave the continent.

The elders who passed these stories on knew and were convinced that the fathers of tribes were giants of prodigious force. They had tried to tell the European explorers who had come to them in the eighteenth and nineteenth centuries of the surprising feats celebrated in their name, how with one hand they dammed rivers, their voices were so great that they could call from one town to another, and birds took flight in panic whenever one of them would cough. Their hunting expeditions drew them far from their dwelling. In a single day they would go hundreds of miles, and the animals they killed, hippopotami and elephants, were carried easily on the shoulders of these fortunate hunters; their weapons were bows from trunks of palm trees; even the earth bore their weight with difficulty.

To quote Robert Goldston, author of *The Negro Revolution:* "No Homeric bard could have better sung the mighty prowess or god-like majesty of the ancient Greeks before Troy." And the old myths and legends of Africa are not unlike the epic poems of ancient Greece. They tell of times before the dawn of written history when heroes trod the trembling earth. But also like the Homeric epics, the tribal legends of Africa were dismissed as cunning fantasy by the first outsiders who heard them. They were not believed by white explorers, missionaries, or traders, not simply because they were recited like myths, but also because it was necessary for the white conscience to believe that Africa had always been the "Dark Continent," comprised of Africans and ignorant savages to whom the benefits of "civilization" were now being introduced for the first time. But just as archaeological research was to establish the veracity of Homeric epic, so modern scientific investigation has begun to establish the amazing truth behind African legend.

About one hundred miles down the Nile from the modern city of Khartoum, capital of the Sudan, lie the sand-strewn, gigantic ruins of a city that flourished more than 3,000 years ago. This is Meroe, capital of the ancient kingdom of Kush. Great pyramids mark the site, and within a few miles of the city ruins stand trampled down temples, palaces, and monuments of a civilization that was famous throughout the ancient world. The Greek historian Herodotus knew of Kush and its famed Temple of the Sun, and so did the pharaohs of Egypt, who traded with the Kushites, conquered them from time to time, brought them the civilized techniques of smelting iron, and learned, in turn, the art of working electrum (a natural alloy of silver and gold). The records reflect contact between Egypt and Kush and Carthage, Arabia, and even Rome.

These "records" are not, of course, entirely written (in stone); they are derived from styles of sculpture, shards of pottery, and a great deal of informed speculation. But although the language of Meroe has yet to be deciphered, the archaeological evidence beneath the sands is definite. It tells of a mighty kingdom whose origins are lost in the midst of antiquity, and it tells of a people who, while they learned much from their northern and western neighbors, taught them much, too.

When the European and American slave traders and invaders assaulted Africa during the centuries following the Portuguese landings at Benin in 1472, they were assaulting an old and by no means primitive civilization.

The coming of European power to the African continent had much the same impact on its developing culture as the invasions of the Huns had on ancient Rome and the incursions of the Mayans and the Norsemen on feudal Europe. To the question, "Why did not African civilization progress after the coming of the Europeans as it had evidently progressed before?" an African might well reply, "How far would European civilization have progressed after the thirteen century had the Mongol hordes of Genghis Khan conquered the entire continent?"

Truth Marches On

Up until 1960, there was a tendency in all media to identify the American experience with only the white American experience and to call the experience of white Americans the history of America. Even today most history textbooks project a white tribal image to a multinational reality. Within recent years, the noticeable changes are a result of the work of black historians and the direct action of black demonstrations. Because of the action efforts of John F. Kennedy and Martin Lurther King, Jr., the Constitution of the United States and millions of other dedicated Americans, blacks and other ethnic groups are witnessing for the first time, on a minimal scale, long overdue rights, for the racial exploitation is brought to a confrontation with truth.

John and Martin were men who set goals that pushed fears aside to tell the world what the United States was really about. Both said in their own way that if this country is worth living for, then she is worth dying for. Dr. King's "I Have a Dream" message was spoken for black people not to lose faith in the American dream, but to prepare to cover the bet that black forefathers placed before stealing away home to be at rest. This, of course, was at a time when they were not sending a message of an attempted break for freedom from slavery. But at that time, they had envisioned a band of angels literally coming to carry them home. One thing was for sure: no matter how we relegate the old Negro spirituals, the slaves that labored under hard bondage and the crack of the slave driver's whip were not less human than we are today, who want the best for our children, even better than we had it. They said: "I got shoes, you got shoes, all of God's chillun got shoes, when I git to heaven I'm gonna put on my shoes and I'm gonna shout all over God's heaven." Since this is a blessed hope for true Christians all over the world today, with all of our modern conveniences for living, shouldn't the ones for whom life was hardest desire a haven of rest? Notwithstanding, they saw beyond their field of labor, through the annals of time the dawn of a new day, just as Dr. King did in his "mountaintop experience."

John F. Kennedy left the words of his inauguration speech ringing in our ears: "Ask not what your country can do for you; ask what you can do for your country." With that now famous speech of January 20, 1961, which called for a national dedication to a worldwide struggle against the forces of tyranny, poverty, disease, and war, the hearts of American people were captured. John F. Kennedy used to say, "The journey of a thousand miles begins with a single step." He took that step at a time when he had the opportunity to do more than talk—the same approach that Martin Luther King, Jr., was destined to take also.

Looking back, it is hard to believe that from January 20, 1961, to November 22, 1963, only two years and eleven months had passed. Sen. John F. Kennedy and his beautiful wife left their home at 3307 N Street, N.W. for him to be inaugurated to the presidency of the United States of America. That N Street address now is a tourist attraction in the oldest section of Washington, near the place of my birth.

Georgetown is the name, and today the Georgetown Hoyas of Georgetown University are the fame. The six-foot eleven-inch giant black coach John Thompson has led this team to a phenomenal championship record in college basketball. Notwithstanding, famous Georgetown was founded in the year 1751, two years after Old Town (Alexandria, Virginia), the old stomping grounds of George Washington and Robert E. Lee, which has more standing houses that date back to the eighteenth century than Georgetown.

Nevertheless, this is where the Kennedys lived before going into the White House. The Kennedys have left an indelible mark not only on Georgetown, but the entire city of Washington.

The nation's capital, with a black majority, has always had Negroes who were business- and professional-minded. As early as 1830, Alfred Lee opened a grain and feed store at 2906 M Street, setting a record over 162 years ago. There were some failures—like the old National Benefit Insurance—and the Masons had a hard time saving their building. That did not stop others.

In this city, Negroes do many things besides work for the federal, state, and city governments. Blacks own and operate many kinds of businesses. Young blacks, unlike their elders, who stuck to the tried and true lines and professions, are not afraid to try the unusual today. Washington blacks in business reap millions. The Hamilton brothers have had a printing plant in the same spot since 1908, closing only when both served in World War I. West was a colonel and taught military science at three Negro colleges. In forty years of business, McGuire's Funeral Home had handled over twenty thousand funerals, including that of the Liberian minister's wife. Their automotive equipment numbers over 160,000. Cobb, Howard, and Hayes was once the best known law firm in the city of Washington, D.C.

On Prospect Street, next to the Prospect House, is the Joseph and Rose Kennedy School of Ethics Institute. Not far from the Watergate is the John F. Kennedy Center for the Performing Arts, and just across the Potomac by way of Memorial Bridge are the final resting places of John F. Kennedy and his brother, Sen. Robert F. Kennedy. On Thirty-Sixth Street, between N and O streets, is the church the Kennedys attended, and where they exchanged their marriage vows. It is also the place John F. Kennedy attended his last church service.

Chapter IV
A One-Thousand-Day Chronicle of John F. Kennedy

On the morning of January 20, 1960, shortly after 8:30, John F. Kennedy and his wife, Jacqueline Bouvier Kennedy, along with Secret Service men, went to a special mass at Holy Trinity Church on Thirty-sixth and N streets, N.W. He arrived at 8:55 A.M. and was met by Fr. Richard J. Casey, pastor of the church at that time. The next series of events were all scheduled for Kennedy.

He was pronounced in excellent health by a medical examiner. A medical report was issued just two hours before he was sworn in as president of the United States of America. Pierre Salinger read a one-sentence statement signed by Dr. Eugene J. Cohen and Janet Travell of New York, who had long been Kennedy's physicians. It read: "A physical examination showed that President Kennedy's health remains excellent."

United Press International disclosed the accounts of events in the following manner: "John F. Kennedy became the nation's 35th president today and called America to reborn greatness, and for a new U.S. and Russian quest for peace." At forty-three years of age, the youngest man and first Catholic ever elected to the presidency, he took his oath of office. Chief Justice Earl Warren administered the rights before an overcoated crowd of thousands from all over the world. A few feet away, head bared, shoulders still erect and squared, John F. Kennedy took his oath of office. The new president and his First Lady then settled themselves straight in their car for the ride down Capitol Hill to the White

House, waving to a half million people along the Pennsylvania Avenue parade route. The crowd also paid moving tribute to outgoing Dwight D. Eisenhower, the retiring president.

In Kennedy's brief, almost unprecedented inaugural address, which at times took on the appearance of a prose poem, he told his countrymen that our task is great: "In your hands, more than in mine, will rest the final success or failure of our course." The single pervading dominant specific in Kennedy's first speech as chief magistrate was his fervent urging for a new quest for peace. "Let us begin again remembering on both sides that civility is not a sign of weakness and sincerity is always subject to reproof. Let us never negotiate out of fear, but let us never fear to negotiate."

Probably never did a president's inaugural speech look less to the plains and valleys west of the Allegheny Mountains and so almost wholely to the land beyond the seas. There was no sharp word of castigation for political enemies, no spoilmen's promises for those who had made his victory. At times, the message held in spirit almost the quality of an epistle from the New Testament; three times Kennedy mentioned God and once the prophet Isaiah. The new president's oath was taken on a Catholic Douay Bible, handed down by one of the Kennedy grandmothers.

The Soviet Union had welcomed the end of the Eisenhower administration and had begun to look at the newly inaugurated President Kennedy for a turning point in Soviet-American relations. UPI released a special communique from Havana, Cuba, on January 1, 1961 stating that Fidel Castro had offered to make the first move in restoring friendly relations between the United States and Cuba. In a balcony speech to 1,000 militiamen, he made a cautious proposition to settle the difference between the two nations, but said that his nation would remain militarily prepared in case threat of imminent aggression reappeared. He had blamed the Eisenhower administration for the tension between the two nations but stated that the change in administration would help Cuba, even though he did not expect any radical moves by Kennedy. Castro emphasized that his immediate policy would be to "watch and wait."

After listening to the gracious words of the new president, we were all hopeful that the promises made that day were more than political rhetoric and that they would become a reality. Judging from the conversation of the people that hired my cab that day, it would seem that most were favorably impressed with the new chief magistrate's inauguration speech. I recall the conversation of a couple of fellows who had put in some overtime working the night before on the snow emergency crew. They had worked most of the night cleaning away the snow from the Pennsylvania Avenue parade route. It sounded like this: "Whatcha think 'bout dis new man in the White House?"

"Oh, I can't say for sure, but he may jus do all those things he said that he would."

"Yep, sounds like a good man from what he's sayin', say he gon git dis country movin' again."

"Well, dey all says that 'til they gits in there ya know, then dey change jes like the weather."

"But he also didn't seem to be jivin' in his speech today."

In most of the hard core areas, the consensus was the same, even along the Fourteenth Street strip where the hustlers are usually indifferent to politics. There was that "time will tell" look expressed in the mood of the people.

The new administration celebrated well into the night, visiting the Mayflower and the Sheraton Park hotels and a party at the home of columnist Joseph Alsop, who lived on Dumbarton Avenue, N.W. The president arrived there at 2:00 A.M. He did not get to his new home at 1600 Pennsylvania Avenue, N.W., until 4:00 A.M. Mr. Kennedy seemed to thrive on the hectic inaugural activities of the day, but Jacqueline had to limit herself from too much participation as she was still recovering from the

Caesarian delivery of her son, John F. Kennedy, Jr., on November 25. The first lady passed up some functions and the inauguration balls shortly after midnight. But for Mr. Kennedy, it had been a long one. Following the oath-taking ceremony at the Capitol, his inaugural address, and a formal luncheon, he and Mrs. Kennedy rode down the avenue at the head of a mile-long parade. Police Chief Robert Murray estimated a crowd of 1 million lined the parade route.

The Kennedys watched the parade from a reviewing stand at the White House. The new president remained for the entire three and one-half hours that it took for the marchers to go by, but the first lady retired to the White House after a half hour. Mr. Kennedy finally got to the White House at 6:15 P.M. He popped out again at 8:00 P.M. to attend a buffet meal at the house of cooperation manager George Wheeler, whose wife thus scored a major triumph. The first lady did not accompany the president, but he returned to the White House at 9:40 P.M. to pick up his wife to do the rounds of the inaugural balls. Mr. Kennedy had gone to all of them; one of them he went to twice. The First Lady returned after attending three of the dances.

The entire town celebrated with the new administration. All over town there were parties, uptown, downtown, and across town. I directed my cab in every direction in accommodating people who were caught up in the gala festivities. As I drove across Thomas Circle and crossed Fourteenth Street on one occasion, there was a group of people who were talking about the new president's speech; one was quoting parts of it while the others roared with laughter and approval, saying, "Yeah, dis man gonna make a change . . . Is you wit' dat?" They were living it up even finding fun in the words that promised a change. In Kennedy's inaugural speech that day, he had used measured phrases in issuing both an invitation and a warning to the communists: "Whether now friend or foe, to begin again with America the search for peace." But in so doing he declared, "Let every nation know whether it wishes us well or ill, that we shall pay any price, bear any burden, meet any hardship, support any friend or oppose any foe in order to assure the survival of liberty." The forty-three-year-old president almost bluntly drew attention to his comparative youth in pledging to fight for liberty and to defend the rigths of man.

"Let the word go forth from this time and place to friend and foe alike," he said, "that the torch has been passed to a new generation of Americans born in this country, tempered by war, disciplined by a hard and bitter peace, proud of our ancient heritage and willing to witness or permit the slow undoing of those human rights to which the nation has always been committed and to which we are committed today at home and around the world."

He drew a strong response from the crowd when he asked if the people were ready to join in an effort to forge a worldwide alliance "North and South, East and West against tyranny, poverty, disease and war!" "Yes! Yes!" the throng roared back, and it was outgoing President Eisenhower who led the applause when Kennedy solemnly declared, "My fellow Americans, ask not what your country can do for you, but ask what you can do for your country. My fellow citizens of the world, ask not what America will do for you, but what you can do for the freedom of man."

The following day after the administration and the celebrating until 3:30 A.M., President Kennedy plunged into his first work schedule in the White House with an important meeting on administration grounds and talking with his political command. The new chief executive, displaying campaign vigor, had crisscrossed the nation's capital, attending a series of inaugural balls. It was a long and exciting day, said he, as he climbed to the White House North Portico with vigor at 8:00 A.M., planned lunch with the Democratic National Committee at 1:00 P.M., and presided at the swearing-in ceremony of his cabinet members at 4:00 P.M. and that same day was expected to attend a banquet at the Alfalfa Club. The swearing-in ceremony depended upon quick work by the Senate, the cabinet appointees, and United Nations ambassador designate Adlai Stevenson, who were expected to win confirmation at an unusual Saturday session.

That busy first day schedule indicated that the youthful, active president would move swiftly in putting his "New Frontier" into high gear. Mr. Kennedy had taken his office only the day before as the thirty-fifth president of the United States of America, and immediately challenged the Soviet Union to join in a "Quest for Peace" and had gotten an early response to his plea. Soviet ambassador Mikhail Menshikov was interviewed by television reporters at the big inauguration ball at the Nation Guard Armory. He said he felt that the Kennedy speech marked a turning point in Soviet-U.S. relations. From Moscow, Premier Nikita Khrushchev sent a congratulatory message expressing hope for a "radical improvement" in Soviet-American relations.

The new president had begun to live up to all of his campaign promises; he was off and running in the direction of getting the United States moving. And in the city of Washington, D.C., where the Kennedys lived, there was new life. For the first time since Franklin and Eleanor Roosevelt left the White House had black people shown an interest in what was being said or done by the First Family. And, on the other hand, it was also the first time that a president felt it incumbent to call and encourage a black man while he was fighting against racism in this country.

John F. Kennedy was without question one of the greatest presidents that ever took office. In the brief span of time (one thousand days) of his tenure in the White House, he won the hearts of the people in the nation's capital. The Kennedy years were marred by at least one mistake. He was given no time to grow into his job; pressures of that time were problems that called for his immediate attention. He was given no breathing space in the Cold War—the Communist bloc under the leadership of Nikita Khrushchev pressed for world dominion. February brought crises in Laos. The following day, there was a new crisis in Cuba, where Fidel Castro ruled under communist dominion. On April

15, the United States learned that three B-26 planes, armed by anti-Castro forces, had bombed the island's military airport. The next day it was reported that troops opposed to Castro and trained in the United States of America had invaded Cuba's Orient Province. Actually, the invasion had occurred elsewhere, in the Bay of Pigs.

President and Mrs. Kennedy, like many other American families, watched the flight of our first astronauts from take-off on their television sets at 1600 Pennsylvania Avenue, N.W., which flight made him the pioneering president of the Space Age. Because of his decisions of bravery at home and abroad, he quickly became a courageous hero at home and around the world.

The United States was at the brink of war as the result of a confirmed government report of existence of ballistic missile bases in Cuba that were being constructed with the assistance of the Soviet Union. That condition posed a threat to most of the North American continent and could reach as far as Lima, Peru. "Until these missiles are dismantled, and the flow of offensive weapons stopped," said the president, "it shall be the policy of this nation to retaliate in response to the Soviet Union for any nuclear missile launched from Cuba against any nation in the Western Hemisphere. This shall be regarded as an attack on the United States requiring such action."

President Kennedy became a world hero. He began his third year in the White House as a leader who gave hope to the world that more peaceful times lay ahead. True, as far as the Cold War with the Soviets was concerned, areas of deep unrest remained and others would soon develop. Soviet troops and technicians, still stationed in Cuba, troubled many Americans when the U.S. military en route to Berlin were delayed at Soviet checkpoints. Those actions scarcely promoted friendly negotiations. And we became involved against Communist guerrillas in South Vietnam, where we stood firm for the rights of the smaller nations of Southeast Asia to choose their own government. Yet despite these point of stress, the feeling continued that even Khrushchev looked with growing respect upon Kennedy as a force to be reckoned with in the world and that, therefore, prospects for future harmony between East and West had brightened.

Kennedy called boldly for a new approach to problems dividing the great power block—new hope, new thinking, new action was the sign of the Kennedy appeal, his formula for leadership in international affairs, and Khrushchev responded cordially to Kennedy's overtures. That summer, the signing of the limited test ban treaty by the United States, the United Kingdom, and the Soviet Union was hailed as a first step toward that more secure future for which so many yearned. John F. Kennedy, confident, young, and strong, was their symbol of faith. As he visited West Germany and Ireland that summer, thousands of Europeans cheered him.

The year of 1963 will also be remembered for a series of events in history that began in Birmingham, the largest city of Alabama and long known as the capital of segregation to most blacks. There in Alabama, wherever and whenever the cancerous sore of racism erupted, President Kennedy administered the healing balm. Although President Kennedy and Dr. King did not always agree on time as far as life, liberty, and the pursuit of happiness were concerned, I think it is safe to say that they both held the same views.

Under the leadership of Dr. King, president of the Southern Christian Leadership Conference, and Fred Shuttlesworth, President of the Alabama Christian Movement for Human Rights, guaranteed under the existing federal laws, Eugene (Bull) Connor, commission of public safety in Birmingham and a champion of segregation, led a violent reaction. Police dogs were turned on demonstrators. Heavy water hoses swept people from the streets. Children were treated as ruthlessly as adults, and the spectacle of this merciless treatment revealed by television cameras sickened the nation.

By early May, more than 1,000 demonstrators, of which at

least half were black and under eighteen years of age, had been jailed. President Kennedy intervened, believing that he had secured a truce by which both sides could negotiate sensibly. Three days later, the home of a leader of black demonstrations was bombed, setting off even worse riots. A crowd of better than twenty-five hundred blacks attacked the police. Bricks and bottles flew through the air. Cars were overturned. Six stores and a two-story apartment house were demolished. Fifty persons were injured. President Kennedy stationed federal troops near Birmingham, and gradually the tension eased.

Thus began the so-called Negro Revolt of 1963—the most militant uprising by black people since the days of the Civil War. (Though the Civil War was not a black revolt, the freedom of the slaves resulted).

The hearts of the people the world over were chilled by incidents such as the bombing of a Negro Baptist church in Birmingham where four little girls were killed and several children attending Sunday school were injured, the shooting death of the white civil rights crusader Viola Liuzzo, walking from Attalla on a road in Alabama from Tennessee to Mississippi; and the shooting in the back of Medgar Evers, a leader of the National Association for the Advancement of Colored People in Jackson, the capital of Mississippi. The North, no less than the South, was showing increasing resistance to Negro demands for full citizenship, and in the White House Kennedy faced a problem the severity of which no president had known since Abraham Lincoln. These two men, the sixteenth and thirty-fifth presidents of the United States, both had approached the problem of the Negro from the same base, hoping that education and moderation would solve the racist and human problems involved. Both grew older and wiser and more abashed, because they recognized the struggle. Lincoln, within his lifetime, before he was assassinated, took the first step, freeing the slaves, even though reluctantly, for there was no place for the Negro to go at the time; not even the clothes on his back were his. Nevertheless, Lincoln signed the document that would allow blacks to grow to full citizenship. In 1963, after a full century, John F. Kennedy came to the realization that he too must face the facts, that no matter what his decision might be, it could cause him to suffer and ruin his political future. In this spirit, on June 19 to be exact, the president addressed a special message to Congress. ". . . Birmingham's tragedy should have taught the nation," he said, "that the results of continued federal inaction would not only continue but increase racial struggle." He submitted to Congress proposals on civil rights in three areas:

1. In facilities related to interstate commerce—hotels, restaurants, stores—all citizens should be guaranteed equal rights.
2. Where citizens were denied their civil rights, especially in cases of school desegregation, the U.S. District Attorney should be empowered to bring suit on behalf of these legally injured individuals.
3. Work supported by federal funds should provide vocational training for Negroes until they were qualified to hold such jobs.

Not since Lincoln had any president struck so hard or at greater political risk for the quality of life for all Americans, not at the typewriter, but at the White House from his rocking chair. Kennedy, in so doing, added a new chapter to his *Profiles in Courage,* a book that he was affiliated with, if not the author—one that depicted the heroism of great Americans of past history.

President Kennedy had gone further than any other president before him in becoming personally committed to the passage of the Civil Rights Bill, by giving more support than ever from the White House. That summer of 1963 became known as the Civil Rights Summer, with Dr. King at the head of a movement growing ever stronger, to the point of making black citizens more aware of their political rights. Because of white oppression or black apathy, tens of thousands of Negroes had never voted or even registered to vote in many of the farming towns all over the South. The civil rights campaign was meeting fierce opposition from extremist groups and from ordinary whites who could not accept that the days of white domination were numbered.

Chapter V

The Historical Wake

On Friday, November 22, 1963, the headlines of the *Evening Star* in Washington, D.C. read: "PRESIDENT IS KILLED BY SNIPER IN DALLAS, TEXAS."

The paper said in bold headlines that President John F. Kennedy, 35th president of the United States of America, was shot to death today by a hidden assassin armed with a high powered rifle. Mr. Kennedy, 46, lived about thirty minutes after a sniper cut him down as his limousine left downtown Dallas, Texas. Reporters said the shots that hit him were fired about 12:30 P.M., Eastern Standard Time. A hospital announcement said that he died at approximately 1:00 P.M. of a bullet hole in the head.

Automatically, the mantle fell on Lyndon Baines Johnson, a native Texan, who had been riding two cars behind the chief executive. In Washington, an air force officer said that he understood that Mr. Kennedy's body would be arriving at Andrews Air Force Base in Maryland at 5:25 P.M., Washington, D.C., time. Assistant presidential press secretary Malcolm Killduff said Mr. Johnson was not hit, as previously reported.

Mr. Kennedy died at Parkland Hospital, where he had been taken in a frantic, but futile, attempt to save his life. Lying wounded and in serious condition at the same hospital was Gov. John Connolly of Texas, who was cut down by the same fusillade that ended the life of the youngest man ever elected to the presidency. The First Lady had cradled her dying husband's blood-smeared head in her arms as the presidential limousine raced to the hospital. "Oh, no," she kept crying. She was not hit, but Governor Connolly slumped in his seat next to the president.

Shortly before Mr. Kennedy's death was known to the public, he was given the last rites of the Roman Catholic church. He was the first such president in American history. Even as the two clergymen hovered over the fallen president in the hospital's emergency room, doctors and nurses administered blood transfusions—it appeared to be hopeless. Mr. Kennedy died of a gunshot wound in the brain at 1:00 P.M. Eastern Standard Time, according to the announcement by Mr. Killduff.

Police ordered an unprecedented dragnet of the area in search of the assassin. They believed that the fatal shots were fired by a white man about thirty years of age, slender of build, and weighing about 165 pounds, standing about 5' 10" tall. The murder weapon reportedly was a 30-30 rifle.

The new president, Lyndon B. Johnson, and his wife, Lady Bird Johnson, left the hospital a half hour later. The reporters had no opportunity to question them. The horror of the assassination was mirrored in an eyewitness account by Senator Yarborough, a Texas Democrat, who had been riding three car lengths behind the president. "You could tell something awful and tragic had happened," the senator told the reporters before the president's death became known, his voice breaking and his eyes red-rimmed. Senator Yarborough went on to explain, "I could see a Secret Service man in the president's car with his hands up in angry anguish and despair. I knew then something tragic had happened." Senator Yarborough had counted three shots from a rifle as the presidential limousine left downtown Dallas through a triple underpass. The three shots were fired from above a triple underpass, possibly from one of the buildings or bridges, or even from the grass. One witness told television reporter Mal Couch that he had seen such a gun emerge from an upper story window commanding an unobstructed view of the presidential car.

In a window, watching, waiting, stood the assassin, with rifle raised, firing three shots, wounding Governor Connolly and killing President Kennedy. The paper said that it was allegedly Lee Harvey Oswald.

That day in the city of Washington, D.C., time stood still. People were leaving their jobs with and without permission. Many were weeping openly, others grimaced from the pain that the horrible news bore, and it continued to flood the airwaves as more and more of the gory details came in. People from all walks of life were shocked into mourning. Suburbanites, sociologists, black militants, political figures, revolutionaries, entertainers, speed freaks, dope dealers, newspapermen, writers, policemen, and what have you, all of these formed the swirling vortex of mourners that I watched through the windshield of my cab on November 22, 1963.

Chapter VI
The Aftermath

Later that evening, following the assassination and after having put in a hard day driving people who were, like myself, shocked, saddened, and dumbfounded, I picked up one passenger going to National Airport. We rode down Seventeenth Street, N.W., and passed the Washington Monument to our left. We were reaching the point where the road veers to the right and curves left to the entrance of the little bridge—that is, if you are going into Virginia, as we were. Under normal circumstances, the tour guide in me would have seized the natural opportunity to talk about the black architect and bridge builder Archie Alexander, who was commissioned in 1942, a year before Franklin Delano Roosevelt dedicated the Jefferson Memorial, for there is no place in Washington more beautiful around the last of March and the first of April, when the Japanese cherry blossoms are in bloom. All these reflections I had submitted to memory that day. Besides, my passenger seemed only interested in reaching his destination, and I knew from experience when to oblige. The news of the tragedy had left precious little to be discussed that chilly November day.

At the airport as I discharged my passenger and waited for the fare, I had noticed quite a confusion of people and newsmen gathering and pushing to get close to the center of attraction. I later found out it was none other than Dr. Martin Luther King, Jr., who had just arrived on one of the many flights to Washington that day. Having had my fill of surprises for one day, I left the airport bound for home. Later via television I saw and heard Dr. King responding to a question from one of the reporters, saying, "This is what happens when hatred goes unchecked or when there is a climate so filled with hate, ignorance, and fear." Ironically, five years later, this man who advocated peace was to fall victim to the same fate under similar circumstances.

In the case of John F. Kennedy, newspaper editorials had created a climate so filled with hate and ignorance that any number of bigots could have pulled the trigger that stopped the world and set America back only God knows how far. With Martin Luther King, Jr., the same was true, along with the fact that he was disturbing the establishment as few black men had before him. The exception in his time was Malcolm X, a contemporary who was far more militant in his philosophy. One was the apostle of integration and the other a dynamic apostle of separation. Both men came from deeply religious backgrounds, the Negro Baptist church, and they had sat in the pews as their fathers preached. They both caused divisions among the very people they had dedicated themselves to reclaim.

Following the Kennedy assassination late in 1963, Malcolm X made a statement referring to it by saying, "The chickens come to roost" (which I will go into later). While all the world was mourning the loss of our thirty-fifth president, Malcolm's statement came forth like a cog in the wheel of history.

Shortly after the assassination was learned of there were Buddhist prayers offered in Tokyo, Japan. In Berlin, Germany, twenty-five thousand mourners marched to the courthouse, assembling in a square soon to be renamed John F. Kennedy Plaza. In London, among the other signs of sorrow, the Union Jack flew at half-mast over Parliament. In France, Spain, Italy, and every other place of any size and every other country around the world, people burst into tears at the news of the young president's death. Some held solemn church services. In Rome, Pope Paul VI, filled with heartbreak, buried his face in his hands. From all around the world, every corner of the globe, messages were sent with condolences and expressions of love for a young president whose life had been so needlessly wasted. In New Ross, Ireland, from which the first Kennedy left to come to the United States, a sobbing priest said, "Never again will we see his smiling face." How, why, could anyone so young, a man who had served so short a time in the White House, so move the heart of all the world?

In Washington, D.C., all who attended the funeral services or watched on television saw some of the reactions of a grief-stricken world. Among them were Prince Phillip of England, Prince Bernhart of the Netherlands, King Boudouin of Belgium, President Macapogal of the Philippines, Emperor Haile Selassie of Ethiopia, and Pres. Charles de Gaulle of France. They all gathered at John F. Kennedy's final resting place in Arlington Cemetery, a place John F. Kennedy had picked himself one day while he, Chief Justice Warren, and friends were in Arlington for a wreath-laying ceremony. John F. Kennedy had remarked, "This must be one of the most beautiful spots on earth."

That day, while the funeral was in progress, prior to going to Arlington, I had the privilege of revisiting the statue in the little park across from the church. I read the words on top of the statue, describing the ancient order of the Hiberians: "They comforted the dying, nursed the wounded, and carried hope to the imprisoned. Gave in His name a drink of water to the thirsty." They were fitting words for those who paid the supreme sacrifice for the betterment of mankind, and they gave impetus to those who, by example, took up the Cross and followed Christ's example. The very thought added to the nostalgia of that moment as I left to watch the mourners come out of the church.

Chapter VII
No Alternative to Nonviolence

The sympathizers of the negative sound of the Malcolm X statement concerning the assassination were the radicals who basked in the climate of hatred that encouraged the assassination, whose children cheered the president's death in their classrooms. Minutes after the news of the assassination circled the globe, the nation was gripped with fear and grief that lingered like a cloud over the nation. Here in Washington an unknown dread and fear showed on the faces of the people. The big question was, What next? Will the radicals take over? Kennedy had dealt with the racial crises at a point that called for justice, for it is at this point that laws must be passed to create a climate for justice. From a scriptural point of view, laws cannot create a climate for love; that is not what they are supposed to do. But from the same point of view it is love that transcends law and not law that transcends love. The truly born-again believer in the Bible seeks always to balance love and justice. The main foundation of truth in the Bible is that God is love. "For God so loved the world that He gave His only begotten Son that whosoever believe in Him should not perish but have everlasting life" (John 3:16).

God's great demonstration of love was His son, Jesus, the only begotten Son of God who had no other earthly ambition than to do the will of God, the one who had sent him. God is a good God because He is a just God; a just God blesses and prospers the obedient and all who are pursuant of His promises just as the disobedient and the unjust reap bitter fruit for the error of their ways.

The charge that President Kennedy was killed by the work of hate groups was never proven to be fact, but too many in this country expressed joy at the end of the Kennedy days. The big question here is, How can the crises in human relations be solved through a type of Christianity that has become identified as the white man's religion, reflecting faith in scientism, secularism, and racism? On the other hand, what could be expected from establishing a black religion? Would it be less self-centered than a white religion? Martin Luther King, Jr., once responded to a similar question by saying, "One tyranny is no greater than another where choice is the question." In regard to the statement made by Malcolm X during a question-and-answer period following one of his speeches, commenting on the assassination, he said, "These were not made as an expression of joy, but to point out an existing situation that has plagued black people since the country began." The exact transcript of what Malcolm X said in reply has never been published. What was reported was that Malcolm X said, "The chickens come home to roost." The public press was remembering still Malcolm's concept of God slapping down a plane loaded with white southerners as retribution for the killing of Black Muslims in Los Angeles, and reporters interpreted Malcolm's comment as a statement of jubilance over Kennedy's death. The press was justified in the handling of Malcolm's remarks. He literally invited misinterpretation by saying, "Being an old farm boy myself, chickens coming home to roost never made me mad; they've always made me glad." When he was asked what was the reasoning behind his remarks after the assassination of the president or was that an instance for rejoicing, an instance of chickens coming home to roost, he said, "Yes, but let me clear up what I said. I did not say that Kennedy's death was a reason for rejoicing. That is not what I said at all. Rather, I meant that the death of Kennedy was a long line of violent acts, the culmination of hate and suspicion and doubt in this country."

"You see," said he, "this country has let white people get away with killing and brutalizing those they don't like. The assassination was a result of that way of life and thinking. The chickens come home to roost—that's all there is to it. America at the death of the president just reaped what it had been sowing."

Malcolm X at the time was under orders from the Honorable Elijah Muhammad, head of the Black Muslims, of which Malcolm X was a member, not to make comment on the assassination. Yet he did so in open defiance of that order, which resulted in his being put on suspension and ordered not to speak publicly until further notice. Malcolm's disposition on this matter stemmed from his erroneous belief about his religion, God, and Muhammad, the man he had chosen to follow. He had placed a reverential trust in a man and had become indoctrinated by him, with many of the ideas that he had then harbored: ". . .the white man was the devil and . . . separation from him was black America's only recourse." Being the impulsive speaker that he was, Malcolm could not resist the temptation to speak for the public record when questioned about the assassination. Like Martin Luther King, Jr., he was the son of a Baptist minister.

Malcolm's father was Earl Little, whose gospel had a mixture of Christianity and Garveyism—the notion that the American black man would never find peace in this country and thus should return to Africa. *The Autobiography of Malcolm X* gives an indepth report of Earl Little and how he was chased from town to town because he had discussed white racism. White vigilante groups opposed to his preaching had persecuted the Little family from town to town and Mr. Little from one odd job to another. While the Little Family was in Omaha, Nebraska, they were visited by the Ku Klux Klan, who came and galloped on horseback around the house, screaming a demand that Earl Little come out, perhaps to be killed. It so happened that he was not at home but away on a preaching mission in Milwaukee, Wisconsin, at the time. Mrs. Louise Little had no alternative but to stand up for her tormentors so they could see that she was with child; she stood in the doorway in full view, in the light of the moon. She explained to them that her husband was not at home. Then Louise

Little returned to her children, but the whites did not immediately leave the house. Instead, they continued to gallop around the house, screaming the dogma of white supremacy and smashing the windows with their guns until every pane of glass was in fragments. Then, with torches burning high, they rode off into the night.

Earl Little returned home and was contorted with anger to hear and see what had occurred in his absence. A black man at that time had but one recourse—flight. But Earl Little elected not to pick up and move to yet another town, to yet another job, until his wife gave birth. The period of waiting was a time of reflection for Earl Little. The violence and family disruption that menaced him were merely a continuation of the pattern that had plagued him and his family for years. Little was born in Reynolds, Georgia. He had six brothers, three of whom were killed by white men, one of them lynched. The same fate most likely would have awaited Earl Litlle had he remained in Omaha.

Then in May 1925, the child was born. They named him Malcolm Little. He was successively to be named or called Big Red, Malcolm X, and finally El-Hajj Malik El Shabazz. The family moved to Milwaukee for a period, but Earl Little's search for economic independence from the white man caused him to move to Lansing, Michigan, where he bought a home and planned to open a grocery store. However, it was just a question of time (a few months) before he was in trouble again, with the white establishment of Lansing. Malcolm explained that his father had committed the sin of wanting to own his own store in the area outside the Negro district and spreading unrest among the good "niggers" of the town. Once again, violence lashed out at the Little family. In *Autobiography*, Malcolm described the events in these terms.

> This time, the get-out-of-town threats came from a local hate group called the Black Legion. They wore black robes, instead of white. Soon, everywhere my father went, Legionnaires were

reviling him as an uppity nigger for wanting his own store in the Negro district of Lansing, for living and spreading unrest (Garveyism) and dissension among the good niggers. In 1951, Earl Little was found dead with half his skull smashed in. The murder was never solved, but the conviction among the blacks was that the Klan beat my father unconscious and then placed him there on the streetcar tracks where the car all but cut his body in half. With the funeral began a six-year effort to hold the family together.

This was a case so typical of the besieged black family. As no social alchemist could be found to remedy the situation in that day for the Little family, the same holds true today for most blacks, Hispanics, and other American people; we must realize that if our democracy is to survive, we must all strive to make it one that will one day be equal to its earlier contribution to mankind: a democracy of white men. The destiny of this country is tied up with the destiny of black people.

In 1832, Alexis De Tocqueville, a distinguished young Frenchman, sailed for home after an extensive nine-month tour of the United States. Though he was not as sure as he had been at one time that democracy would prove suitable for his native land, he returned to France with a genuine appreciation for the way it worked in the land he had visited. He saw only one dark cloud on the horizon. "The most formidable of all the ills that threaten the future of the Union," he wrote, "arises from the presence of a black population upon its territory." The two nations or races, he pointed out, were alike, but are unable to entirely separate or combine, though they were attached to each other without intermingling. Today, one hundred years and a civil war later, we have not found a suitable way to satisfactorily integrate the Negro population into general society, although it has been tried in almost every conceivable way.

Racism is as rampant in the United States as it ever was because Christianity, in its pure and true form, alone can make the difference, but not as a white man's religion; if it reflects faith in scientism, secularism, and racism, it distorts the true call of the Bible for all men to be saved: "Turn to me and be saved all the ends of the earth! For I am God, and there is no other" (Isaiah 45:22). If the issue was religion, having a set of values that best suit an individual's life, then we all know that the white man's set of values cannot possibly solve the black man's problems. As a matter of fact, these values are the very ones that keep these problems from being solved.

Christ's mission was to "seek and to save that which was lost," to redeem individuals from the curse of sin. As he bore witness to the truth, his promise is as it was: "You shall know the truth and the truth shall set you free." The truth, where the racial crisis is concerned, then, is that bigotry, hatred, and prejudice rest in a transformation of the individual through Jesus Christ. The true Christian is called upon to recognize and to direct his message to both the institutional and personal prejudices in his quest for justice; race or color has nothing to do with it.

Over a hundred years ago, Frederick Bremer, a European visitor, told white Americans, "The romance of your history is the fate of the Negro." As long as the United States has a racial crisis, we cannot in good faith dictate policy to the world on human rights, as a people that holds the solution to the world's ills. Racism at this point and time in history is like using fog lights on the wrong road. If one is doing that, plus traveling the wrong road, naturally one should slow down and get one's bearings because the surroundings are different and things are seen under a different light. In such a case, quick thinking will tell a good driver to turn on the high beam light, for the only thing that can dispel darkness is light. And, in a very real sense, God is the light and the truth is His shadow. The simple analogy is that if you willingly follow the truth (read signs, et cetera), you will stay on the right road. High beams are preferable on rare occasions, but often when used, light is not at its fullest potential. Likewise, half-truth will never do. Think what would happen to our judicial system if all the trials were based on half-truths. We can be thankful for the whole truth, nothing but the truth. Jesus said in praying to the Father, "Sanctify them through thy truth, thy word is truth" (John 17).

Is there not a right and wrong way to think in the pursuit of truth? Is it not right thinking to accept that which is most apt to be right? Is it not wrong thinking to accept that which is least apt to be right? Is not logic the type of reasoning that always accepts that which is most apt to be right? Does not that reasoning that is most apt to be right always eventually lead one to the truth?

The United States is the greatest country to date because of liberty and opportunity, and we have more potential for doing good than any other country on earth. But we are not where we ought to be as a nation, though we began on the right road by recognizing God. The so-called Pilgrim Fathers came to this country seeking the freedom to worship God as they wished. To this day, engraved on our "most prized possessions" are the words: "In God We Trust." But the United States is not where she ought to be in terms of faith in the Constitution or God, who inspired its writers.

Chapter VIII
American History Complete and Unabridged

The black history of America began in 1619, one year before the landing of the *Mayflower,* when a ship with no name, with twenty-four blacks aboard, landed in Jamestown. The captain's name was Jope, and there was an Englishman whose name was Marmaduke. The notable couple were Isabelle and Anthony. Those first black settlers were not slaves. As a matter of fact, this was fifty years before the slave system began in the colonies. Although black history is the essence of the American experience, and, indeed, we are created by that history that followed our pilgrimage here in this land, from a black perspective we know that this country was not always run by a system of color caste by which the communities were divided.

There was a time when black and white indentured servants worked together in the same fields and lived together in the same huts. They played together in the same fields after working hours and, of course, they mated and married. So widespread was the intermingling during this time that Peter Fontane and other writers said that the land swarmed with mulatto children.

The years 1619 to about 1660 were a period of primary importance to American history. Americans worked out their terms of servitude and were freed. Within a few years, Negroes accumulated property, pounds, and indentured servants. One Negro immigrant, Richard Johnson, even imported a white indentured servant and held him in servitude.

The developing bonds of community between black and white Americans began with a conscious decision by the white power structure of colonial America. In the 1660s, men of power decided that human slavery based on skin color was to be the linchpin of the new society; this would provide a larger labor force, which was needed for the thriving growth of the cotton and tobacco plantations.

Indians were often sickly and had a knowledge of the countryside that made it easy for them to run away. If all indentured servants were enslaved, that would have presented a problem. When a white escaped, for example, he could easily blend with the rest of society. Also, since most white servants had been Christianized, it was very difficult to justify enslaving another. One other important factor that made it difficult to enslave white men is that usually they were subjects of strong European governments to which they could appeal for protection.

Blacks, on the other hand, were strong, healthy, visible, cheap, numerous, and unprotected. When men in power made their decision, they were forced to take other ominous steps, since nature does not prepare men for the role of master or racist; the rigid training began and persisted while hearts grew even more callous and cold. In order to make men deny other men and women and themselves, this must be the case. Men must be carefully taught to hate, and the lesson learned by one generation must be learned by the next.

The Negro and white working class of the 1660s—the bulk of the population—had not been prepared for roles outlined in the new script of the statutes. It was necessary, therefore, to teach them that they could not deal with each other as fellow human beings. How was that done? It was done by an assault on the Negro's body and the white man's soul. Legislators ground out laws of every imaginable description, and vigilantes whipped the doubtful into line.

Behind the night riders, of course, stood God himself in the person of Parson, who blessed the rupture in human relations with words of the Bible. The Bible was used then much as it is today, in a way that the thought implied is a lie. Who was responsible for this policy? The planters, the aristocrats, the lawyers, the Founding Fathers . . . the good people: men who would say later that there is a natural antipathy between Negro and white America, but the record belies them. Negro and white Americans were taught to hate and fear each other by words, sermons, whips, and signed papers and lies agreed upon. The process continued over a period of more than one hundred years, which saw the Negro family and the exclusion of the Negro worker from one skilled trade after another.

Nor did white men escape. They saw dimly what they were doing to themselves, and they drew back from themselves, afraid. But they did not stop—perhaps they could not stop—for by now racism had become central to their needs and to their identities. Moreover, they were moved by dark and turbulent forces within. The evidence of their need bred fear and guilt and additional demands for exclusion and aggression. Propelled by this dynamic, the whole process of excluding and fearing reached something of a peak in the first decade of the twentith century, with a carnival of Jim Crow in the South and a genteel movement that blanketed the North with restrictive covenants. The net result was a system of color caste that divided communities, North and South, into mutually hostile groups. Since that time, investigators have focused almost all their attention on the Negro community, with the resulting neglect of primary determinants on the white side of the racial line. Asserting that the Negro problem is a predominantly white problem and, as it has been suggested, anything that hides the white American from a confrontation with himself and with the fact that he must change before the Negro can change is still a major part of the problem. This was the finding of the National Advisory Commission on Civil Disorders.

On July 29, 1967, President Johnson appointed a special group of distinguished Americans, under Gov. Otto Kerner of Illinois, to research the root cause of the problem of militancy during the summer of 1967 in Newark, Detroit, and Cleveland and across the nation. The finding was that the deep-rooted, bitter dissension stemmed from the result of over three hundred years of inequities visited upon black people as second-class citizens. If these problems are to be solved, it will be when men take their fate out of the hands of men and place it in the hands of Christ: "Blessed is the nation whose God is the Lord" (Psalms 33:12). And again, Christianity in its pure and true form alone can make the difference here. I will say again that the white man must swallow his pride and seek forgiveness for his racist attitudes that have caused the racist crisis. And the black man must forgive in a true demonstration of Christian love. When man, as an individual, finds his own peace with God, making peace with his fellowman will follow naturally. Where there has been a genuine transformation of an individual through Jesus Christ, bigotry, hate, and prejudice must come to an end.

In *The Autobiography of Malcolm X,* his life as a youth growing up in the city typifies that of many thousands of youths who are plagued by racism at an early age in life. It is natural for a black kid without a father image to rebel against society when that society harasses him rather than helping him to find himself; Malcolm's family life was shattered with the death of his father. Following a series of ordeals he became a hustler and eventually went to prison, where he became acquainted with the Black Muslim doctrine and consequently came to embrace the father-teacher image under the teaching of Elijah Muhammad, who preached a doctrine that summed up all of Malcolm's crystallized thoughts. On the Sunday before Labor Day in 1952, Malcolm Little, who had come out of prison on parole only a few weeks ago, was received by the Hon. Elijah Muhammad, leader of the Black Muslim organization and a very strong role model for the son of Earl Little. Early in January 1953, Malcolm gave up his job in order to devote more time to the Black Muslim movement, and that summer he made the journey to the pulpit, as he became the assistant minister of Temple No. 1 in Detroit.

In 1958, Eric C. Lincoln, a professor of religion and sociology at Clark University in Atlanta, was alarmed at receiving a term paper from one of his students that stated: "The Christian religion is incompatible with Negroes' aspirations for dignity and equality in America." The paper began by pointing out the fallacy of the Christian religion, saying that it has separated believers on the basis of color and hindered where it was morally bound to be forthright, as it had declared its mission to a universal brotherhood under Jesus Christ. The paper also stated: "Christian love is the white man's love for himself and for his race. For the man who is not white, Islam is the hope for justice and equality in the world." It ended up saying: "We must build for tomorrow."

Lincoln, himself a Christian clergyman, was startled by what he read. Investigation revealed that his student had become a convert to the Nation of Islam through the activities of the minister in charge of Temple No. 15 in Atlanta. Lincoln's curiosity and scholarship led him to obtain a grant and return to Boston University and complete his doctorate; his dissertation was the first scholarly analysis of the Black Muslim movement.

Louis E. Lomax, a personal friend of Malcolm X, was preparing a television documentary on the Black Muslim organization in 1959 and crossed paths with Lincoln, who was researching and preparing his book, *Black Muslims in America*. Both famous authors are responsible for most of the knowledge that we have about the Black Muslims. When Malcolm X began to do his evangelistic work as a minister of Islam, he taught and reverberated what the Honorable Elijah Muhammad had delivered in all of his messages found in the issues of *Muhammad Speaks*, which is a Nation of Islam publication. Some years later, I began to read and to study the Holy Quran, which is the Bible for about 725 million worshippers of the Islamic religion, and I have found that the publication contains very little of the Holy Quran that admits the deity of Jesus Christ. No one else that ever lived has successfully proven the claim of having risen from the dead. Christ did, and the empty tomb in Jerusalem confirms that claim. One must settle this question if Christ is to become Lord and Savior.

If religion is a felt practical relationship with what is believed in as a supernatural being, then to me Christ is all that he claimed to be. One day, I asked myself this question: If Christ is more apt to be the Son of God than he is not, then how can I refuse to accept him? The evident answer led me to salvation. After all, the world has seen fit to date time from his birth and death and to admit the greatness of his teachings. I considered it a wise move to personally accept his being the Son of God and my personal savior. I had determined that to me he was either the Son of God or he was the greatest blasphemer, fake, and liar that the world has ever known.

Are not all things either more apt to be right or more apt to be wrong? If this be true, then are not all the teachings of Jesus more apt to be right than wrong? Also, is not all teaching that is contrary to the teachings of Jesus more apt to be wrong than right? If this reasoning be good logic, then how can one follow that which is more apt to be wrong, which would cause a person to accept that which is more apt to be wrong than right? Will not wrong thinking lead to wrong acts, resulting in wrong ends that are to our detriment? How can we neglect to accept that which is more apt to be right?

Malcolm X, in his brilliant autobiography, explained his religion and his dedication to a man. He had risen from being a pimp, dope peddler, thief, hoodlum, and hustler to become one of the most dynamic spokesmen of the black revolution, but he failed to realize that truth has no religion. Neither can it be channeled in its entirety through doctrines of men. Malcolm explained, "I had more faith in Elijah Muhammad than I could have in any other man on the face of this earth." When that man let him down, he was hurt, bewildered, and forlorn, as he had to pick up the pieces and seek out the truth of the Islamic religion and its relation to his life. From 1952 to 1964 Malcolm had been dedicated to the Muslim religion; he built the organization by winning new converts and building new temples. He left that movement in 1964 to organize Muslim Mosque, Inc., and later the nonreligious Organization of Afro-American Unity. He made two trips to Africa and Asia, including Middle East, during 1964. Three months later, he was assassinated in New York, on February 21, 1965. Malcolm X was a speaker, not a writer; when he spoke people listened. After he was silenced by the Hon. Elijah Muhammad, it had become clear to him that his long-awaited reinstatement was fruitless. He then began to speak to the needs that all black people have in this country. He was black manhood, speaking his peace to racist white America.

Malcolm X, like Martin Luther King, Jr., being well acquainted with the history of black people, was able to speak the truth about the new methods of exploitation that are used on blacks. And racist white America began to get the message. Malcolm X was invited to speak at colleges and universities all over the United States because zeitgeist demanded an audience for the voices of black America. In a speech to a militant black audience, he emphasized the need for black unity, "Message to the grass roots." Malcolm X said, "We all agree tonight that America has a problem and that we, the black people, are the serious problem. The reason that she has a problem is because she does not want us here." He also said that each time we look at ourselves, whether we are black, brown, red, or yellow, a so-called Negro, we represent a person who possesses such a serious problem for America because we are not wanted; once we face this fact, then we can start charting a course that will make us appear intelligent. "What you and I have to do," Malcolm said, "is to forget our differences when we come together. Baptist or Methodist, neither do we catch hell because of being Democrat or Republican, Mason or Elk," and he added, "and we sure don't catch hell for being an American; because if you were an American you wouldn't catch hell." He went on to say, "We all catch hell for the same reason, because we are all black, so-called Negroes, second-class citizens, ex-slaves." Then he quipped, "You don't like to be called that, but what else are you? You didn't come here on the *Mayflower*. You were brought here by people who came on the *Mayflower*, or the so-called Pilgrim Fathers." Malcolm explained, that black people have a common enemy, oppressor, and exploiter and common denominator. But he said once we realize that we have a common enemy, then we unite on the basis of what we have in common.

He said that what we have foremost in common is that white man who is an enemy to all of us. I know that some of you think that some of them are not enemies; time will tell.

In April 18–24, 1955, in Bandung, Indonesia, the Bandung Conference of African and Asian nations took place on the site of West Java Province, Indonesia. In the interior of Java on the northern edge of a plateau nearly twenty-four hundred feet above sea level, is the city founded in 1810 by the Dutch. In the mild and pleasant climate surrounded by rice fields and waterfalls is Bandung, a modern city with wide, tree-lined streets and many buildings and residences built in Western style. It was here that African and Asian nations took a strong stance against Western colonialism. In all, twenty-nine countries representing more than half the world's population sent delegates. The new *Encyclopedia Britannica* exploits the legacy in revealing many wrongs that were set right at this meeting. A good example is the major debate, centered upon the question of whether Soviet policies in eastern European and central Asia should be censured along with Western colonialism. A consensus was reached in which "colonialism in all of its manifestations" was condemned, implicitly censuring the USSR as well as the West. The conciliatory Chinese attitude tended to quiet fears of some anti-communist delegates concerning China's intentions. A ten-point "declaration on world peace and cooperation" incorporating the principles of the U.N. Charter and Jawaharlal Nehru's Five Principles, was adopted unanimously.

Malcolm X made reference to the Bandung Conference saying that it was the first meeting of black people in centuries and that what happened at the conference and the results of that conference are a model for the same procedure you and I can use to get our problems solved. He pointed out that at Bandung all the nations came together, the dark nations of Africa and Asia, and that some were Buddhist, some of them were Christians, some of them were Confucianist, and some were atheist. But despite their differences of religion, they came together. All of them were black, brown, red, or yellow.

The number one thing Malcolm said that was not allowed was the white man, explaining that once they kept him out, everybody else came right in and fell in line. This is the thing that you and I have to understand. And these people who came together did not have nuclear weapons, they didn't have jet planes, they didn't have all the heavy armament that the white man had, but they had unity.

They were able to submerge their petty differences and agree on something, that one African came from Kenya and was being colonized by the Englishman, another African came from the Congo and was being colonized by the Belgian, another one came from Guinea and was being colonized by the French, and another came from Angola and was being colonized by the Portuguese. When they came together at the Bangdung conference they looked at the Portuguese and the Dutchman and realized that what they all had in common was that they were all from Europe, they were all Europeans—blond hair, blue eyes, white skins. They began to recognize who the enemy was. The same man that was colonizing people in Kenya was colonizing the people in Congo. The same one colonizing the Congo was colonizing people in Kenya, South Africa, Southern Rhodesia, Burma, India, Afghanistan, and Pakistan. They realized that all over the world the black man was being oppressed by the white man; the dark man was being exploited by the white. So they got together on the basis that they had a common enemy.

It is evident from the speeches that Malcolm X made that he had a deep understanding and insight to the problems in most of our cities. He also understood the cunning craftiness of the white power structure to deceive, manipulate, and frustrate any cause directed at black unity. The reason black unity has been consistently discouraged in this country is the white man's fear of having to compete on a footing of equality. From the very beginning it was the white man's fear of the black man, fear of slave insurrection, fear of loss of property, and fear of what life would be like without slave labor. Black history tells us that black people survived in this country only because we pooled our pennies and nickels and created a record of collective sharing that is one of the wonders of the modern world. Had not the Woodsons and the Duboises preserved our records we would be locked into the present and certainly tempted to believe the lies that black people won't stick together and black people won't work and prefer Welfare to honest labor. The history of black people tells us that no one in this country is owed more for the work they did for two hundred years from sunup to sundown without pay.

Though Malcolm X was opposed to nonviolent rights demonstrations, in his fiery speeches he drove his messages to the hearts of his audiences. He finished one message with an appeal that black people

> stop quarreling among themselves, go into a huddle, don't let the white man or enemy know you've got a disagreement. Instead of airing our differences in public, we've got to realize that we're all the same family and when you have a family squabble, you don't get on the sidewalk—if you do, everyone calls you uncouth, unrefined, savage. If you don't make it at home, you get in the closet, argue it out behind closed doors, and then when you come

out on the streets, you pose a common front, a united front. That is what we need to do in the community, and in the city, and in the state. We need to stop airing our views in front of the white man, put the white man out of our meetings and then sit down and talk shop with each other. That's what we've got to do.

The Black United Front and the Black Caucus found direction from Malcolm's prophetic philosophy.

The three sectors of society by which slavery was upheld were religious, economical, and political. They saw slavery as a divine institution, ordained by God; so it was preached and taught by white pastors who quoted from Genesis the story of Noah getting drunk and naked and how Ham's descendant, Canaan, was cursed by Noah for mocking him. Ham was black (the Hebrew definition of *Ham* was "black"); therefore, God had cursed all black people and relegated them to a condition of servitude. But it was Noah, in a drunken stupor, doing the cursing—not God. As I have stated before, God is a good God, because he is a just God. He sees the disobedience and the unjust punished as surely as He rewards and blesses those who are obedient to His word in the Holy Bible.

Unless we turn to God and receive forgiveness for sin, the Scriptures declare that God has set before us a blessing and a curse: a blessing if we do the will of God and a curse if we do not. The blessings and the promises of God are to His children who have been born again through His Son, Jesus Christ. They are also conditional to one's faith in God and one's conformance to His will and according to His time. When all Christians in the United States will seek justice, righteousness, and truth, then we will hear and understand His words: "If my people which are called by my name will humble themselves and pray and seek my face and turn from their wicked ways, then will I hear from heaven, and will forgive their sin and will heal their land" (2 Chronicles 7:14).

I believe that Christianity is the answer to the racial crisis in the United States, but it must be pure religion and undefiled. We must see one another as brothers and realize that we are our brother's keeper. We must forget the past and plan together for the future, which will be neither black nor white in the sense that we know it now. Although most whites think of the United States as their country without regard to black America, they know full well that we were here from the beginning, shared in all of her struggles, and shed our blood that she might be free. From slavery until today, black people are asking themselves, "Didn't I plant dem taters—didn't I plant dat corn, didn't my folks before me fight for dis country before I was born?"

Chapter IX
The Revolution

Malcolm X made a few remarks about the difference between the black revolution and the Negro revolution, asking the question: Are they the same? And if they are not, what is the difference? First, what is the difference? First, what is a revolution? Sometimes I am inclined to believe that many of our people are using this word *revolution* loosely, without taking careful consideration of what the word actually means and what its historic characteristics are. When you study the historic nature of revolutions, the motive of revolution, and the methods used in a revolution, you may change your mind.

Look at the Revolution in 1776. That revolution was for what? For land. Why did they want land? Independence. And the only way they could get it was through bloodshed. There was no love lost, no compromise, no negotiation. I am telling you that you don't know what a revolution is, because when you find out what it is, you will get back in the alley and get out of the way.

The Russian Revolution, what was it based on? Bloodshed. And you are afraid to bleed. I said you are afraid to bleed. As long as the white man sent you to Korea, you bled. He sent you to Germany; you bled. You bleed easily for white people, but when it comes to seeing your own churches being bombed and little black girls being murdered, you haven't any blood. You bleed when the white man says bleed, you bite when the white man says bite, and you bark when the white man says bark. I hate to say this about us, but it is true. How are you gonna be nonviolent in Mississippi and Alabama? Your churches are being bombed and your little girls are being murdered, and at the same time you're gonna get violent with Hitler and Tojo and somebody else you don't even know. How can you justify being nonviolent in Mississippi, as violent as you were in Korea?

If violence is wrong in the United States, violence is wrong abroad. If it is wrong to be violent in defending black women and black children and black babies and black men, then it is wrong for the United States to draft us and make us violent in defense of her. If it is right to make us violent in defense of her, then it is right for you and me to do what is necessary to defend our own people right here in this country.

The Chinese revolution: They wanted land. They threw the British out, along with the Uncle Tom Chinese. Yes, they did—they set a good example. When I was in prison (you're still in prison; that's what America means—prison), I read an article in *Life* magazine showing a little nine-year-old Chinese girl. Her father was on his hands and knees, and she was pulling the trigger because he was an Uncle Tom Chinese. When they had a revolution over there, they took a whole generation of Uncle Toms and just wiped them out, and within ten years that little girl grew up and became a full woman. No more Toms in China, and today she is one of the roughest, toughest, and most feared countries on the face of the earth by the white man because there are no Uncle Toms over there.

Of all our studies, history is more qualified to reward our research. And when you see that you've got a problem, all you have to do is examine the historic method used all over the world by others who have had similar problems to yours. Once you see how they got theirs straight, then you know how you can get yours straight. There has been a revolution going on in Africa—in Kenya, the Mau Mau were revolutionary; they were the ones who brought the word *Uhuru* to the fore. The Mau Mau were revolutionary; they believed in scorched earth; they knocked down everything that got in their way, knocked it aside, and their revolution was based on land, a desire for land. In Algeria, in the northern part of Africa, a revolution took place. The Algerians were revolutionary. They wanted land. France offered to let them be integrated into France. They told France to hell with them. They wanted land, not some of France. And they engaged in a bloody battle. So I recite these revolutions' stories, brothers and sisters, to show that you don't have a peaceful revolution. You don't have a turn-the-other-cheek revolution. The only revolution where the goal is loving your enemy is the Negro revolution. It's the only revolution in which the goal is a desegregated public toilet—you can sit next to white people on the toilet stool. That's no revolution. Revolution is based on land. Land is the basis of all independence. Land is the basis of freedom, justice, and equality.

The white man knows what revolution is. He knows that it is worldwide in scope and in nature. Revolution is sweeping Asia, is sweeping Africa, and is rearing its head in Latin America; the Cuban revolution—that's a revolution. They overturned the system. Revolution is in Asia. Revolution is in Africa, and the white man is screaming because he sees revolution in Latin America. How do you think he will react to you when you learn what a real revolution is? If you did, you wouldn't use that word.

Revolution is bloody. Revolution is hostile revolution—knows no compromise, overturns everything in its pathway. And you, sitting around like a knot on a wall, say, "I'm gonna love these people no matter how much they hate me." No, you need a revolution where you lock arms as Reverend Cleage was pointing out, beautifully singing "We Shall Overcome." You don't do that in a revolution. You don't do any singing—you are too busy swinging. It's based on land. A revolution wants land so the revolutionaries can set up their own nation. These Negroes aren't looking for any nation—they're trying to crawl back on the plantation. When you want a nation, that's called nationalism.

When the white man became involved in a revolution in this

country against England, what was it for? He wanted this land so he could build up or set up another white nation. Malcolm X, at the start of his mission, was revolutionary in every sense of the word. It is plain to see from the things that he said and did with the intention of reaching the objectives of black people who fought, bled, and died for this country. This way of thinking served the purpose of that time; it was an alternative to nonviolence, complacency, and acceptance of continued second-class citizenship for black Americans and their children.

During the summer of 1967, there were black rebellions in many major cities of the United States, all being very similar. Blacks attacked the nearest symbols of oppression: white-owned stores and the police. That summer's rebellion had been preceded by a significant one in New York's Harlem in 1964 and by the Los Angeles Watts rebellion in 1965, which is historic because it seemed to be so carefully planned. In block after block, lone black-owned stores were left standing amidst rubble of burnt-out white-owned establishments.

This was the pattern of the 1967 riots, and to the young militants of the movements these outbreaks were a signal of greater unrest to come, even of revolution to come. There is, moreover, widespread recurrence of the notion that America's problems can only be solved by redistribution of wealth and power in the country by revolution.

Partly this belief in the necessity of revolution results from the failure of the ideal of integration and the unity displayed by black communities in rebellion, which movement leaders had not anticipated, that has helped produce the feeling that radical change is possible.

This feeling has been reinforced by increased contact with and concern for the struggle of people outside of the United States, sparked particularly by the Vietnam War. American Negroes have shown interest in Cuba's revolution, and young people have traveled there and to Africa and Hanoi. The number who participated in the Cuban International Conference is small, and the effect of this new internationalism is not yet predictable. The mood, however, is clear.

James Baldwin in his book *The Fire Next Time* wrote that there is no possibility of a real change in the black man's situation without the most far-reaching and radical changes in the American political and social structure. To this I readily agree, but I cannot lose faith at this point of the journey in the efficacy of the Constitution of the United States or people, black or white, regardless of how slothful or unwilling some have become to envision or effect the changes.

What Malcolm alluded to in speaking of the plantation was a composite picture of the situation of the Negro in this present time by the comparison to the house Negro who lived so close to the master back in slavery. So complacent had he become in his dilemma that he spoke of his master's problems in pluralistic terms: "What's the matter, boss . . . we sick?" Or if the master's house caught on fire, the house Negro fought harder than the master to put out the fire. Malcolm went on to explain that there were house Negroes now as then; he said if there ever was a question of separation, the house Negro would look at you and say, "Man, you crazy? What you mean, 'separate'? Where is there a better house than this? Where can you get better clothes than this? Where can I get better food than this?" That was the house Negro. In those days, he was called a house nigger, and that's what he is called today, because there are still a lot of house niggers running around here. The modern house nigger loves his master. He will pay three times as much as the house is worth just to live near his master—and brag about it: "I'm the only one out there." "I'm the only one on my job." "I'm the only one in the school." You're nothing but a house Negro, and if someone comes to you right now and says, "Let's separate," you will say the same thing now that the house nigger said on the plantation: "What? Where you gonna get a better job than you got here?" I mean this is what you say: "I ain't lost nothing in Africa." Why, Mister house nigger, you left your mind in Africa.

On the same plantation there was the field Negro. The field Negroes were the masses. There were always more field Negroes than there were Negroes in the house. The Negroes in the field caught hell. They ate leftovers. In the house, they ate high on the hog. They call it chitterlings nowadays. In those days, they called them what they were: guts. That's what you were—gut eaters. And some of you are still gut eaters. The field Negro was beaten from morning 'til night; he lived in a shack and wore old cast-off clothes; he hated his master; he was intelligent. That house Negro loved his master, but that field nigger remembered he was in the majority and hated the master.

When the house caught on fire, he did not try to put it out; that field Negro prayed for a wind, a breeze. When the master got sick, the field nigger prayed that the master would die. If someone came to the field Negro and said, "Let's run," he would say, "Anyplace is better than here." You've got field Negroes in the United States today. I'm a field Negro. The masses are field Negroes. When they see this man's house afire, you don't hear the little Negroes talking about our government being in trouble.

In the speeches that Malcolm X made, he gave graphic illustrations of black people in certain positions as a result of racist tokenism, especially in some of our leading cities. A good example in Washington, D.C., which now boasts a Negro majority and a black mayor. In the fabulous Gold Coast and the surrounding areas of Shepherd Park, black people live a life-style that makes them oblivious to the struggles of the field Negroes in the city of Washington.

Out of a population of over eight hundred thousand, there are about five hundred thousand blacks, of whom over two hundred thousand are unemployed. Chocolate City, as it is known among most young blacks, is at least two-thirds black, and in times of trouble, like the riot following the King assassination, the black majority was drawn together, as in war, with a common goal and a common enemy that they could name. War brings people together and gives them exactly what they want out of life: a personal feeling of satisfaction. The federal city has always held a special place in the history of black Americans, because of the one-time existence of slavery in the very shadows of the world's foremost democracy, Washington, D.C., became the one focus of debate over the South's "peculiar institution." The abolition of the slave trade in the District of Columbia comprised an important part of the compromise of 1860. During the war, Abraham Lincoln authorized compensation and emancipation for the slaves of Washington, D.C. In the postwar period, the capital city began to accumulate an increasing Negro population where, despite a southern atmosphere, former slaves found some opportunity. Later in the twentieth century, Washington blacks became a primary beneficiary of better racial practices by the federal government.

According to historians, Washington, D.C., in 1870 had a biracial spirit. In 1860s, the colored people were riding the Washington and Georgetown Street Railroad; they were going to schools run by Quakers and a certain number of Catholic priests. Miss Constance McLaughlin Green, a Pulitzer Prize winning historian who once lived on Capitol Hill, met with the American Historical Society in the Shoreham Hotel and, taking a long look over her shoulder, she said, "In 1867, Congress passed a special civil rights bill for the District of Columbia." Miss Green suggested to the assembled delegates of the annual meeting that "those long dead citizens of Washington, white and black, soon learned to live with the new order of things. They found it less difficult than expected. By 1870, much of Washington, D.C. had become bi-racial in spirit."

"Why was the southern town of Washington so willing? Did she jump or was she pushed?" Miss Green asked. And she concluded that there might have been a shove to where Washingtonians were willing to go. And the era of good racial feelings withered. Why? In 1880, Congress took away the district's home rule and gave it in exchange a promise to pay some of the municipality's cost. The loss of suffrage wiped out the strongest prop. Once the political rights vanished, the Negro rights disappeared. From 1901, the Negro steadily lost ground. There was segregation in the federal government offices by 1904, and by 1913 it was a policy. By the 1920s, the Negro could still sit anywhere on a streetcar and, though there were no public schools for the children, they were still separate. He was a little better off than he'd been in 1862. James W. Silver, the celebrated professor from the University of Mississippi, who had the unmitigated guts to write about that state's "closed society," rose to comment. He said that while there is much to admire, the papers by Miss Green and others were cleverly contrived to prove glorious untruths. They implied that if a few little things had gone differently, we might have solved all our problems one hundred years ago. He said that the people who argued against any civil rights legislation then must be similar to the ones who argue against it now; he doubted that the reception of the civil rights program of the 1860s was really as gentle as Miss Green believed; he said that the climate was certainly worse than it is now, that these are the never, never, people; they say how impossible it is to legislate social inequality for a long time; the difference betweeen now and then lies not in the enemies of civil rights but in its friends. He said that after the Civil War or even during it, the friends of the Negro quit him. Now we have enormous civil rights groups organized and working for the cause. When the people within resist, he said, "The pressure did not agree; it does now and not only can be used, but must be, put on my own State of Mississippi." The restrictive covenants had reached epidemic proportions when the cities across the nation began to explode.

From the year of 1790, when George Washington arrived to pinpoint the exact spot for the location of the permanent seat of the national government, over half of the 753,430 Negroes in the

United States at the time lived in Virginia and Maryland. Thus there was available a considerable reservoir of Negroes, at that time, living in the surrounding areas of the new capital.

Probably the first white man in the area was Capt. John Smith, who came around 1608 and explored the C&O Canal from Great Falls to Cumberland, Maryland. Georgetown, the oldest section of Washington, was founded in 1751, when the rest of Washington was only a city on paper. Originally, Maryland gave 69.25 square miles to form the district while Virginia gave 30.75 square miles to form the federal city. The one hundred square miles was dissolved when Virginia, in 1846, succeeded in having her land returned because of slow development of her portion of the land. Today Washington is comprised of sixty-nine square miles of government land, and government land takes up 45 percent of Washington.

The U.S. Capitol, being the focal point, is located at the exact center of the city of Washington, D.C., on a campsite of the Powhatan Indians. It was later called Jenkins Hill, and today it is commonly called Capitol Hill.

The Capitol faces northeast. Twelve blocks east of the Capitol, in Lincoln Park, stands the Bethune Memorial. On the day of the unveiling of that statue, I had the pleasure of driving the widow of Dr. Martin Luther King to the ceremony. Somehow, following the program in the park, Mrs. Coretta Scott King, one of the members of the black Women's Auxiliary of America, and Mrs. King's bodyguard did not return to the limousine; I assumed that they found other transportation for the parade trip back to the U.S. Capitol. I, nevertheless, was left holding some of Mrs. King's belongings, which I later that day gave to an old junior high school classmate of mine, delegate Walter Fauntroy.

The U.S. Capitol has had 170 years of evolution since its beginning in 1790. The first proclamation by George Washington was to acquire Jenkins Hill. The approach to Washington from Memorial Bridge leading to the Lincoln Memorial is not an inferior view to the approach to London from Westminster Bridge overlooking the Thames River to the Houses of Parliament or the approach to Paris from the bridge on the Seine leading to the place de la Concorde. It has been almost twenty years since I have seen those sites in Europe, but nearly every day, working as a tour guide for the city of Washington, I enjoy this view from the Arlington Memorial Bridge looking to the gleaming white-domed building on Capitol Hill.

The architectural plan of Dr. William Thornton for the Capitol was accepted April 15, 1793, and he was awarded five hundred dollars. The cornerstone was laid on September 18, 1793. When the north wing was finished, the House and Senate moved from Philadelphia, on June 3, 1800, and crowded into it. In 1801, the judiciary moved to Washington. The south wing was completed and joined to the north by a wooden passageway by 1811. On August 4, 1814, the British burned the Capitol. Five years later, reconstruction of the north and south buildings and the new central portion erected cost $2,433,844. The current House Chamber was occupied in 1859.

Much of history has been made in that very place. It was there in 1964, after five months of southern filibuster, that President Kennedy's epochal civil rights measure was passed before crowded galleries there in the Senate Chambers. There on June 26, 1830, Daniel Webster of Massachusetts, then at the height of his powers, rose and answered Robert Haynes of South Carolina in perhaps the greatest speech ever heard in the halls of Congress: "Liberty and Union, now and forever, one and inseparable." Twenty years later, here in the same place, Clay and Webster—now elderly but still giants—put aside their old rivalry to fend off the gathering storm with the compromise of 1850. On March 7, 1850, Webster rose and began the speech that was to bring down upon his head the denunciation of Emerson and Bryant and Whittier: "I speak today for the preservation of the Union. Hear me for my cause." And Calhoun, too ill to speak, declared in an ultimatum read for him that free speech must stop short of agitation against slavery or the Union would end in disunion. I could mention more history-making events that have occurred in that place, but none with more meaning for the future of the United States than the triumph of the Civil Rights March that was culminated with the passage of the measures of John F. Kennedy there in the Senate Chambers of the Capitol. Pres. Lyndon B. Johnson, speaking to an audience at Howard University on June 4, 1965, said "Nothing in any country touches more profoundly, and is more freighted with meaning for our destiny, than the revolution of the Negro American." This man, on whom the mantle of John F. Kennedy naturally fell, did all in his power to see that the bill was passed.

This was one hundred years after Lincoln's Emancipation Proclamation declaring all slaves free in the states then in rebellion against the United States had been signed, on January 1, 1863. This, like a bad joke on black Americans, Jim Crowed its way, lingering over the years until ghettos were firmly entrenched throughout the country, forcing black people into a way of life that was to boomerang ("for whatsoever a man soweth that shall he also reap" [Galatians 6:7]). The sowing of slavery in the United States was the beginning of bondage for both black and white Americans, and at the end of Civil War the troublesome presence of blacks meant the start of more sowing and reaping of deeds that have multiplied in this generation. What must be realized at this point is though we did not all come here on the *Mayflower,* we are in the same boat now.

Today, all America must remember that this great nation began and prospered because we recognized God. The Pilgrim Fathers were in search of a place where they could be free to worship God as they pleased. The words affirming our faith are still on the money: *In God we trust.* These words should serve as a reminder that God is and always has been good to us despite our shortcomings. It is not by happenstance that we are leaders of western civilization; thus far, war has not come to our shores.

We would be wise to return to our first love. The American establishment should take time to consider that God is a just God; He has set before us a blessing and a curse—a blessing if we do the will of God, a curse if we do not. The promises and blessings of God are to His children who have been born into His family or kingdom by His Son, Jesus Christ. They are also conditional on one's faith in God, one's conformance to His will, and according to His time.

Chapter X
Church and State

Jesus Christ reigns in civil society (says the encyclical). When rendering supreme homage to God, society recognizes that it is from him that all authority springs and derives its rights, this fact being precisely what gives authority its sanction and obedience, its imperative character, and its sublimity, also when civil society recognizes in the church those privileges, which it received from its founder, as being a perfect society, mistress, and guide for all other societies. Not that it is the church's wish to diminish the authority of these societies, each of them legitimate within its own sphere, but that she admirably completes them, as grace completes nature.

According to the above papal teaching, heads of state must admit in the first place that all their power springs from God, that is to say from Christ, from whom all sovereignties in this world derive. There is a very definite relationship between church and state, but between the two sovereignties there should be, here in the United States of America, recognition of the universal kingship of Christ, since this is as we quote in our flag salute: "One nation under God indivisible." The eternal salvation of its citizens is not meant to control their religious practices, but it is bound to organize social and economic life in a manner that will enable churches to find full scope.

Were the state to lay aside its secular attributes, it would either come in conflict with the church or else it would lose its own independence. But we must be careful not to underestimate the extent of its sovereignty. In its relation with the spiritual power, the state is not a mere auxiliary charged with material task, a kind of plumber called in to carry out some technical adjustments. No. Although the human order represented by the state does consist largely of material and economic endeavor, it also includes moral and cultural activities.

In this last field, it is true the state's activities were extended by the church in her capacity as guardian of the church's highest moral and religious values. This does not mean, however, that the secular authority is oppressed or absorbed by the supernatural organization. Revelation has not abrogated natural wisdom insofar as this is productive of law, customs, culture, and general principles of morality. All such aspects of civilization on the temporal plane are within the state's competence, no less than is the technical organization of the national life.

Where church and state are concerned it appears that the church has succeeded in hitting upon a happy means of action between two possible dangers—that of losing all contact with the world, so remaining without effect upon it, and that of entering too much into worldly affairs, thus risking a fall from spirituality. History alone will enable us to trace the course of the church's successive experiments and to appreciate its significance. It will help us to see clearly the development of policy through the changing character of world events. History reveals the multitude of moral issues that church should decide, not state, although there should be mutual respect by one for the other. It must be remembered that we the people are the church and that if we are to remain a free nation, we cannot allow the influence of the church upon the state to diminish. The church, after all, is the conscience of the state. To separate religious beliefs and religious conscience completely from the state is to forget that it was belief in Almighty God and freedom under Him that founded that state! The divine authority is higher than the authority of the state; we owe our first allegiance to the omnipresent, omniscient, and omnipotent God who is the light of every man who comes into the world. Dale Evans Rogers, in her book *Let Freedom Ring*, written with Frank S. Mead, said: "To me, the idea of divorcing God from our national life is insulting to God. President Lyndon Johnson in a crucial hour in our history, reminded us that above the Seal of the United States, it says in Latin (translated) *God has favored our undertaking,* I cannot believe God will for very long favor any government or any nation which denies his existence in their midst."

What we have here in America is a religious experience that is not something that comes to a man from an institution that possesses and communicates grace; rather, that institution is formed when religious people voluntarily associate in fellowship and are aware of the presence of the Spirit of God. The aura that attends such fellowship meetings in this characteristic America clearly shows the dominance of the free-church tradition over religious life. The emphasis, in turn, explains the kind of unity between the secular and the religious that has been achieved in the United States of America.

As a nation that began exercising our faith in God we cannot stand idly by while there is an assault on religious freedom in America. Today for the first time in history of this country we have gone on record at the national, state, and local level as taxing churches, imposing fines on churches, and even padlocking churches.

In other words, the governmental institution in our country did not give us religious freedom; it was concern for such freedom under God that gave us our freedom of government. We just can't separate the two.

Ironically in this era we have reached the place where freedom of religion is at stake as arbitrary social demands and government policy invade the First Amendment sanctity of the pulpit.

At such a time when sin is rampant and iniquity is rife, ministers and church officials and members are fined and thrown into jail because of their religious beliefs. Civil and constitutional rights are a federal issue, as we try to extricate our youth from the drugs, pornography, sexual abuse, and murder that are so prevalent in our society.

The annual murder rate in Washington, D.C., alone has soared to four hundred victims, surprisingly over one per day, and most are drug-related violence, not confined to the ghetto areas.

The greatest miracle of the ghettos in the nation's capital is the wealth that is allegedly produced there; fancy cars, gold chains, and diamonds abound in the squalor and stench of the lost horizon of the city. The entourage of visitors that make frequent visits to the ghetto will soon have a ghetto of their own if it continues at the present pace. "What goes around comes around."

Congressman George Hansen published a book entitled *To Harass Our People*. The I.R.S. and Government abuse of power is the theme of the book, which contains a special section, "Assault on Religion."

Chapter XI
The Moral Chagrin of the Churches

When Patrick Henry uttered the thunderous words, "Give me liberty or give me death!" it was for the cause of freedom before the masters of more than four hundred thousand black slaves in the Virginia House of Burgesses in 1775. In the face of one of the grimmest ironies of American history, with the support of several members of the Presbyterians of Transylvania, David Rice, father of Kentucky Presbyterianism, attempted to persuade the State Constitutional Convention of 1782 to prohibit slavery. Rice's address to the convention, including a powerful attack on fantasies about interracial sex, did not, however, carry the day. Three years later, the Kentuckians formally asked the church's highest body, the General Assembly, about the propriety of conscientious non-slaveholders holding Christian communion with slaveholders. The assembly recommended that the parties "live in charity and in peace according to the doctrine and practice of the Apostles," observing that same difference of opinion with respect to slavery that takes place in sundry other parts of the Presbyterian church. In spite of its peacemaking pretensions, the recommendation was thoroughly partisan, since the very point at issue was whether slaveholding was consistent with "the doctrine and practice of the Apostles."

Thereafter, until 1818 the General Assembly repeatedly reaffirmed opposition to slavery while referring the decision on the hard questions back to the presbyteries. Local action was predictably divided along sectional lines.

The synods of the Carolinas, for example, brought their judicial proceedings into line with the secular courts by prohibiting the testimony of their own slave members in their own church courts. The Kentuckians had to face up to their dilemma in 1797 and bring an uneasy peace between antislavery and proslavery factions. The minutes of the Transylvania Presbyterians tell the story. Upon motion, the question was taken up: "Is slavery a moral evil?" It was determined in the affirmative. The question was likewise considered: "Are all persons who hold slaves guilty of a moral evil?" And it was voted in the negative. A third question was proposed as follows: "Who are not guilty of moral evil in holding slaves?" It was resolved that the question now before the presbytery was of so much importance that the consideration of it should be put off until a future day. The future day, of course, was long in arriving.

During the next twenty years, the General Assembly said little. Locally, certain ministries felt compelled to move north and west in order to express themselves freely against slavery. History reveals the proliferation of the slave issue.

Whether or not we dismiss all white southerners as innately evil men, we consider them essentially no different from most Americans. Both their kindness and their hatred can reach limits not approached in most of their countrymen, but they essentially provide mild exaggerations of tendencies common to most Americans. Some are closer to the agrarian way of life, but the nation generally considers itself of people descended from farmers. They are simply Americans of the southern variant with one exception: they live in the area of the nation that was condemned for slave holding and which, due to its refusal to relinquish its slaves, had them forcibly taken away. While it is a clear historical fact that the pertinent reasons behind the Civil War did not include freeing the slaves, still this was the emotional issue offered the public and upon which it waged the war. Out of the conflict there settled over the South the distillate of the viciousness of slavery. Slaves had been held in most states of the Union, but the horror of the system seemed to be connected only with the South.

The quality of cruelty expressed toward blacks became a part of the regional character imposed on the South by the nation at large. In a sense, the United States had cleansed itself of the guilt of slavery at the expense of the principal, but by no means exclusive, offenders.

Here it is not suggested that the adoption of acceptance of this role was entirely passive, for one can easily imagine the embittered losers turning with vengeance on the blacks. Ex-slaveowners may, in fact, have welcomed the role of cruel oppressors, but perhaps, whether it was welcomed or not, they had no choice.

And it is this climate of bigotry, remaining largely unchanged to this day, that surrounds southerners and shapes their attitudes toward blacks. The regional character of the South includes as a dominant theme a contemptible hatred for blacks that reaches irrational extremes.

The atrocities committed by southerners against blacks are carried out by a few, but with the silent assent of the majority. There is no outrage, no revulsion, no call to conscience; rather, there is a tacit agreement that such things happen because of a few "hotheads" who are criticized but are nevertheless protected by the social code. There is agreement that "people feel strongly about such things down here and we do not want outsiders butting in." It is a region with an exaggeration of character, but no more than an exaggeration, for southerners share the American character and their attitudes are to a lesser degree held by all Americans.

A potential for race hatred will be stimulated in any American by the influence of the national regional character. Southerners will become virulent in their hatred of blacks, others less so, but all will hate and fear the ex-bondsmen.

The intensity of antiblack feelings among southerners is such that it cuts across all religious, moral, national, and economic boundaries. Even bonds of kinship give way before the hatred. It is a unique state of affairs when millions of people will conspire and collude to conceal the murderer of a black child. It is monstrous that not one voice was heard to say, "This is the man," when scores of people knew who murdered those black children in a church in Birmingham, Alabama.

William H. Grier and Price M. Cobbs pointed out the fact that of all who have come to the South from all over the world, representing every variation of thought and philosophy, no one has stood up and said, "This is perfidious!" And further, how many religious men have stated from the pulpit that their congregation's behavior is a stench on the nostrils of God? How many philosophers and educators have publicly declared that their neighbors forfeit their claim on humanity by their bestial acts? Of all the millions of southerners, brave and cowardly alike, men who have decried the oppression of blacks (in this case) have been almost nonexistent (William H. Grier, *Black Rage*).

"Thy kingdom come, thy will be done, if I hadn't stole this I wouldn't have none." The feeling is that patois is and has always been the double communication black people use to protect themselves against cheating, slander, humiliation, and outright mistreatment by the official representatives of society. Afro-America's experiences have taught that if the black man does not develop a profound distrust of his white fellow citizens and of the nation, he will live a life of such pain and shock as to find life itself unbearable. For his own survival it was necessary to develop a cultural paranoia in which every white man is a potential enemy unless the black personally finds out differently. The painful experience of Afro-America has taught him to know his tormentor quite well. The sadness and intimacy with misery has become a characteristic of black Americans. It is a cultural depression and a cultural masochism.

With an eye to history, it can readily be seen that language was used with a particular emphasis on double meanings. In fact, multiple meanings were imposed on language, for example, in the spirituals. If it is true that blacks are more likely to steal than whites, William H. Grier and Price M. Cobbs have suggested in their book, *Black Rage*, that there is no more efficient way to produce a thief than to steal a man's substance and command that he hold his peace. Aside from the moral issue, the historical picture makes America's treatment of blacks somewhat exploitative and that exploitation has continued to this very date. When African slaves were brought to this country, they were selected and grouped; in that way, slaveowners sought to avoid communications between the slaves and to prevent conspiracy. In addition, it was forbidden to teach slaves to read and write. They were to learn only the practical language of the field and that from the lips of their masters and overseers. As a result, the slaves learned English as a series of garbled, half-understood, mispronounced words shared mainly by the few slaves on the same plantation. The psychological importance of this device should not be underestimated, for the slaves were even taught to speak by their masters.

However, the slaves turned the language as it was presented to them to their own purposes and, in fact, to the precise purposes that their owners sought to prevent. While the mispronunciation and misunderstandings were a source of great amusement to the slaves' owners, the garbled patois began to be used as a secret language among the slaves. To the uninformed listener the words spoke of religious longing; the singing provided a harmonious accompaniment to their work, and to the viewer all was piety and submission. The true meaning of the spirituals, however, involves a communication from one to another regarding plans for escape, hostile feelings toward the master, and agrarial expression of a rebellious attitude. As the language of any group provides a feeling of identity and group unity, the patois of the slaves came to take on new meaning and purpose for them. But all the while no slaves could deny that his speech remained a badge of inferiority in the eyes of the whites. The slaves turned this badge of their own devices as best they could.

The southern drawl reflects the interaction of master and slave in showing certain aspects of the slave culture. The southern dialect is a slow, leisurely, gracious, often devious meandering around an idea that has scholarly, patient, highly civilized quality about it. At its best, it reflects a way of life involving man's highest aspirations, a passionate devotion to honesty, humility, learning, and compassion. At its worst, it has a brutal, primitive quality that is shocking to other English-speaking people. It is in the latter light that the realities of the slave culture are reflected in the language. In fact, the polarization of attitudes reflected in the language expressed the intense ambivalance of life in the southern United States. The tentative tendentious quality of the language is often used to obscure the inconsistencies in the life of the southerner. Things that cannot be faced squarely are covered over with an obscuring script of softening words.

In later years of slavery, when some slaves were able to master the language and after the emancipation of slaves from bondage, a proliferation of schools enabled large numbers of ex-slaves to learn the language, but still the indirectness of southern language patterns fitted the needs of the oppressed black minority perfectly. In the circumlocution so necessary to the beleaguered blacks, it became a more refined art.

In contemporary Negro life, the patois of old is ubiquitous. Those few highly refined blacks who say they cannot speak the patois do not deny that they understand it thoroughly when spoken by someone else. It remains essentially the language that the black man uses with his fellows and continues to represent years of bondage. In this sense, it is despised and rejected by many Negroes. Thus we can see how the patois has served a wide-ranging adaptive function for black people from the earliest days of enslavement in the United States down to the present. If we are willing to agree that the primary adaptive purpose of the patois during slavery is no longer functional—that is, conspiracies and escapes are no longer discussed in words of double meanings—and if it is also clear that the patois now brands its user with a great deal of negative attributes and if, further, we appreciate the ease with which a more generally acceptable manner of speech can be acquired, we must then look for other explanations for the continuation of the patois in general usage among blacks. Explanations are to be found in the unconscious usages to which such speech is put.

One important unconscious use of this patois rests on the Negro's perception and, in fact, his white confrere's perception as well that the true status of the races in the United States at this time is that Negroes are regarded as slaves who are no longer officially enslaved. In this light, the same attitudes exist on the part of the white majority toward the black minority, and the hostility and aggression that the white potentially feels toward the black must be dealt with by Negroes who seek to live in this country. The patois, then, may continue to serve the purpose it served originally during the period of enslavement. Out of fear and out of the brutal necessity of dealing with a white oppressor, the black American must from time to time convey to the white person that he is aware that he is perceived as inferior—and is at least nominally willing to agree that he is inferior. Thus the patois continues to serve an adaptive function even though the circumstances to which the adaptation must be made are less clear and the nature itself may be unconscious.

Still driven to his verbal depreciation, the black man puts the patois again to his own uses. The "jive" language and the "hip" language, while presented in a way that whites look upon simply as a quaint ethnic peculiarity, are used as secret languages to communicate the hostility of blacks for whites, and great delight is taken by blacks when whites are confounded by the language.

One step removed is the music of Negroes. Black musicians have always sought to express something uniquely black and to express it in a way that leaves whites dumbfounded and excluded. Most popular music in the United States expresses this progressive change in the manner of expression of black musicians. No sooner have some whites learned the special techniques than Negro musicians develop a new, more difficult technique, and when that too can be shared by whites another more complex idiom is developed. Any student of contemporary music can follow this evaluation and will be impressed by the technical and theoretical developments black musicians have produced in response to the drive for a unique and ethnically singular method of expression.

Blacks today continue to follow the patterns of slavery times. By appearing to accept the ethnic stereotypes that are intended to depreciate them, they turn these stereotypes to their own group purpose. The idea that Negroes have natural rhythm was originally used by whites to depreciate any mystical creativity observed by blacks. Today this stereotype is embraced by black people and elaborated in the creation of a singular music that the white cannot create and that he can neither play nor understand. In the concept of "soul," black people agree that they can sing and dance and experience music in a way that whites cannot. The stereotype that Negroes have some kind of animal-like capacity to excel in athletic events is embraced by blacks who say, "Yes, we are stronger, swifter, and more beautifully coordinated than whites."

And as for the stereotypes of the black man's sexual superiority, which has many psychological roots but is offered in a depreciating way as evidence of his more animal-like and less civilized nature, to this black people add an emphatic "Yes!" Thus the patois and the other demeaning attributes are turned to a positive and elevating use and continue to bind black people together with a sense of identity and group solidarity.

Chapter XII
Facing Facts

There are token blacks who have gained fame and fortune. Some have soared above the heights of many of their peers that hail from Europe, Asia, and other parts of the world, who, like their white counterparts, either ignored or evaded the implications of black history and chose to identify with Euro-American history, rather than with the Afro-American struggle. Many black celebrities, for instance, who became independently wealthy and submit to an interracial marriage as a business proposition agree with the old racist concept, "If you're white you're all right, if you're brown you stick around, but if you're black get back." And it goes without saying that "If you have money you can act funny." When you examine the record and the motives behind many interracial marriages, you will have to agree that black people were only good enough to marry caucasian mates if they were rich, famous, or both. At least, this is the way it appears to be. Many times, blacks who all their lives enjoyed the flower garden became famous and yielded to the temptations of picking a wild rose, whose thorns left scars for a lifetime.

All over the United States, of course, today, whites and blacks are becoming color blind. And here in the nation's capital the old game of "cat and mouse" goes on. Whites and blacks who do not associate during the daylight hours often meet in the shadows around the Potomac for a taste of the forbidden fruit. Some became attached to one another and try to make a go of it, only to find that if they insisted upon maintaining the relationship, polite society phonies would frown. Most are not willing to pay the price of being put down because parents and friends would never accept what could turn out to be a wholesome relationship for life.

Since I have been driving taxicabs and limousines throughout Washington, I have met quite a cross-section of folks from all over the world and from all walks of life, at work and at play, the "haves and the have-nots" that all make up the social life of the city that is 45 percent government; the center of western civilization. Here bills are passed into law and visitors are met by the descendants of Colonel Hooker's brigade that once camped out on Pennsylvania Avenue. They parade from Midtown to Georgetown in blue jeans and in satin gowns. They offer to comfort or console the rampant men out on the stroll.

Chapter XIII
The Positive Black Catalyst in Washington

When I was a youth growing up in Washington, D.C., around 1941, names like Officer Oliver A. Cowan had the ring of our famous sports heroes of today who hit a home run, score a touchdown, or make the winning points in the last minutes of play in championship basketball. During that time period, there was not a whole lot to do or a lot of places to go that were of interest to restless youth. Therefore, it was easy for young people to get into mischief or trouble. It was about that time that pocketbook snatching, yoking, and teenage gang fights reached epidemic proportions in Washington. In fact, the area of the Thirteenth Precinct, on Barry Place, N.W., was known as the "Bucket of Blood"; that is to say unless one could defend himself with a knife and draw blood, he did not belong in that neighborhood.

In that area, three individuals had died in the space of three months. Officer Cowan organized the youngsters and decided to do something about the things that were happening in their community. They had come up with a self-rehabilitation program that reduced crime so drastically that the chief of police, the late Mayor Kelly, came to the neighborhood to meet these self-reformed gang leaders. The Junior Police and Citizens Corp., Inc., spread throughout the city and over into Anacostia's Garfield section, where my brother became one of the first mayors in the area. I firmly believe that he found his direction for pastoring the Emmanual Baptist Church there on Ainger Place in Garfield, from his experience as mayor of the Junior Police and Citizens Corp.

Nevertheless, that organization, whose major objective was to get to the source of the juvenile delinquency problems, became so successful that their programs attracted the attention of the editors of the *Saturday Evening Post* and *Look* and *Life* magazines. These were the youngsters whose efforts and examples of self-reform were copied in cities all over the country. Their slogan, "construction instead of destruction," came from the missing thing found in their research. They found that the Thirteenth Precinct had the highest rate of delinquency in the city, but that the boys who gave it that reputation were few in number, although their names constantly returned on the precinct books. It was found that many of the chronic repeaters belonged to the local Boys' Club, the Twelfth Street YMCA, and the Banneker Playground Recreation Program. As a matter of fact, most of the repeaters were the athletes of these institutions. Further investigation revealed that many of these youngsters came from homes that were not broken and many went to church on Sunday, but something was still missing—that missing thing was believed to be moral discipline. Although their energy was used for play, their minds were not used for constructive activities, but rather for destructive activities. Thus the corps slogan, "construction instead of destruction." That slogan became the direction for and the goal of every program that the government was to start following the Kennedy administration and the assassinations.

The United Planning Organization was one that I am very familiar with because in 1967 I was hired as a job coach by Ralph Petey Green, who was in charge of all job coaches at the time. UPO was then composed of people who were mostly from the target areas; some were dying of frustration. Many people in these areas were like driftwood on the sea of life; someone has well said, "A drowning man will reach for a straw."

When money was allocated for the purpose of helping these people (who had no boots, not to mention the bootstraps), people who were not from the poverty areas came and were employed to do what they knew precious little or nothing about. Most of them were hired because they had a college education or they knew somebody who knew somebody, but they knew nothing about poverty. Some had just discovered that they were black; others studied to learn slang—which comes from exposure, not rehearsal. Petey Green was an exception. He was an ex-convict who had been a junkie and was locked up on an armed robbery charge that led to an extended stay in the reformatory. One day when a fellow inmate climbed to the top of the tower to commit suicide, it was Petey Green, with a gift of gab, knowledge of human nature, and experience in the hard places of life, that talked the inmate into changing his mind.

As job coaches, we dealt with ex-cons, drug offenders, school dropouts, hustlers, and people who were living from hand to mouth. The street in the ghetto (the hustlers' world) is viewed as and sometimes referred to as "game," and the "get them before they get you" motto prevails in its self-defeating and self-destructive way. The pimp or the player that controls one or more ladies is aware of the intrinsic danger that he abides under, the ever-abiding shadow of the law. He is always gaming and striving to say ahead of law enforcement in order to keep on making his game. And well does he know that even the ladies of his stable may become ambitious job seekers awaiting a miracle in employment in order to move on to better things, since they are leading "a dog eat dog" life-style. People in the ghetto live according to and in agreement with a book of unwritten law of the game world, and sometimes they are more loyal to one another than some who have professed to be God's children.

The system that built that ghetto and insists on maintaining it is the one that perpetuates the game. When you rob and cheat a man in the democratic process and frustrate his abilities by denying him his rights to function as a normal human being, he is then left with the alternative of employing methods that violate all of the middle-class laws of the status quo and gleefully informing the white middle class where they can shove their value system. As long as ghettos remain and people cannot find the legitimate means to support themselves, the salutations of those who survive by the book will be in like fashion: "Hey, Bruhr! What it look like?" or "Everything is everything! . . . Same ole, same ole." Segregation in the United States has caused divisions between black and white to the extent that not only have Afro-Americans created a language that whites cannot comprehend, but an entirely different social culture right in the midst of white America. It began on the slave plantation, where twofold messages were revealed in song. A deep baritone sang the following words: "Steal ah-way, steal ah-way, steal ah-way to Jesus—steal ah-way home, I ain't got long to stay here." And a high tenor would pick up the chorus with, "My Lord He calls me, He calls me by the thunder—the trumpet sounds within my soul"; then the refrain, "I ain't got long to stay here." The message was complete. And Harriet Tubman led hundreds of blacks to freedom by the "underground railroad."

The parallel today is almost as it was then except that now we are not singing the spirituals that we communicated by and too many are not keeping the faith that this country started out with. The life of stress and frustration has led us instead to become steeped in drug and alcohol abuse to the point where blacks risk all for a shot at affluence and "freedom," which keeps us dodging that giant foot that is taking its toll on black youth hustling drugs rather than working at McDonald's for less money.

Chapter XIV
The Black Freedom Struggle

Black Americans, in the words of Thomas Jefferson, ". . . of right ought to be free." They have more than earned that right to full emancipation. Blacks have been here from the beginning, shared in all of America's experience and drenched this soil with their blood in every war, in defense of her. Crispus Attucks was the first ex-slave to give his life in defense of America—in the Revolutionary War—but far from the last. The blacks who died in the defense of this nation are many and sundry.

The Department of Defense in the Pentagon bears record that by 1865 over thirty-seven thousand black soldiers had died in the Civil War—almost 35 percent of all blacks who had served in combat. This heavy toll reflected the fact that black units had served in every theater of operations and in most major engagements, often as assault troops. Some of those casualties were due to poor equipment, bad medical care, and the "no quarter" policy followed by the Confederate forces facing them. To the black troops themselves, these casualties reflected the great desire to prove to an uncaring nation their great desire for full citizenship and participation after the war. They were fighting to be free, not to return to the plantations as slaves.

The 1963 March on Washington was not only held to let off steam for the thousands of disenfranchised marchers who had come with legitimate grievances, but was Dr. Martin Luther King's moment and monument, although the idea of the march was not originally Dr. King's, for as early as 1941 A. Phillip Randolph of the Brotherhood of Sleeping Car Porters had threatened to lead a black march unless something was done about racial conflicts and discrimination. Franklin D. Roosevelt did not like the idea. Roosevelt said, "What would happen if Irish and Jewish people were to march on Washington?" But in the end he agreed to sign an executive order—creating the Fair Employment Practices Commission. The march was called off. Nevertheless, in 1963 the seventy-three-year-old gentleman of the civil rights movement met in the Brotherhood office in Harlem, New York, with his friend and disciple Bayard Rustin to talk over strategy. Both men were socialist and pacifist. Rustin was twenty years younger than Randolph and had been arrested more than two dozen times for demonstrating against war or racism. He had worked in India with Gandhi, in Britain for nuclear disarmament, and for independence in West Africa. Rustin and Randolph shared the belief that black people can achieve equal rights in the United States if they progress hand in hand with underprivileged whites. Both men agreed that a massive new front was needed to bring home to the people that "the struggle was moving into a new phase."

It was Rustin who reviewed the idea of a march on Washington, and Randolph enthusiastically agreed. But when Rustin showed Randolph the proposal, he said that it would not do: "This is simply a matter of more rights for blacks, and what I want you to go and bring me back is a plan for jobs and freedom." One thing stirs the pride of blacks in America, and that is the desire to be accepted as first-class citizens in this country where we constantly have been told that the time is not yet.

Both Randolph and Rustin knew that in order to get around the Kennedy opposition and the various factions of the civil rights movement they would have to have unity—and that was not easy to achieve. There were, at that time, five civil rights organizations that counted. In theory, they shared the same goals. But that was not always obvious; they had slight but noticeable differences in style, tactics, and ideology, and they engaged in fierce competition over public membership and, above all, fundraising.

The National Association for the Advancement of Colored People (NAACP), led by Roy Wilkins, had a tinge of caution and conservatism about it. Its faith in litigation had begun to turn off younger, more important blacks. But it had a formidable record of solid achievement, including the greatest victory of all, in the Brown school desegregation case. And with its 170 branches it was a true mass organization able to raise a goodly revenue for dues.

The Urban League under Whitney Young was far smaller in leadership than the NAACP. But it was strongly founded, mostly by the white philanthropic establishment, and knew how to work effectively inside the power structure.

The Southern Christian Leadership Conference (SCLC) was regional, not national. It was relatively young and poor, and its leaders were mostly southern black ministers who, while dogged, were inexperienced. But it had shown the power to put massive demonstrations into the streets of southern cities and defy intimidation. It already had incomparable prestige and the charisma of Martin Luther King, Jr.

The Congress of Racial Equality (CORE) came of a secular, more radical tradition committed to direct actions. Though its origins were interracial, middle-class northern as much as southern, under James Farmer and Floyd McKissick it began to strike up a mass support among blacks in some rural areas.

The kids from the Student Nonviolent Coordinating Committee (SNCC) were the guerrillas of the southern direct action struggle. They had no money and precious little else. They fell into several ideologically distinct factions, the two most important of which turned out to be the Nashville group, philosophically committed to Gandhi's nonviolence as taught by theologians like Gandhi, James Lawson, and C. T. Vyvian, and the radical "northerners." Many of them were from Howard University, like Stokely Carmichael and Courtland Cox, who later ran the "Drum and Spear Bookstore" on Fourteenth and Fairmont streets, N.W.

In the summer of 1963, John Lewis, a stocky minister congenial in temperament and nonviolent philosophy to the SCLC people, took over as chairman of the SNCC. SNCC owed its mystique more to two men who stayed in the background. One was the slim Harvard-trained mathematician Robert Parris Moses. The other was tough-hewn Jim Foreman, born in Mississippi and raised in Chicago. Even more perhaps it was the jaunty courage of rank-and-file field secretaries, in their denim overalls, that captured the imagination of southern black sharecroppers and northern white reporters alike. They became a kind of symbol of a whole movement of which they were only one part. Bayard Rustin spelled out the tactics for achieving in a shrewd memorandum: "First Rustin reminisced to someone, if you got King pinned down it would be hard for anyone else to say no. Second, we had to get Wilkins because, with all the things that people say about the NAACP, it is the only group that can organize blacks." Wilkins and Rustin disliked mass demonstrations. But Rustin would also support whatever Mr. Randolph asked him to. Only when Wilkins and King forged an alliance would it be time to turn to the White House liberals—the labor people and the churches.

That part of it worked according to plan. First King, Wilkins, and the other civil rights leaders announced their support, though according to Rustin not before one of them had said under his breath, "Damn that Phil Randolph! If only he had talked to one of us first before putting us in a position where we can't say we aren't going along with these things he wants."

Then labor came in, led by Walter Reuther, and the churches. Eventually a committee of ten leaders of the march consisted of Randolph and the heads of five civil rights organizations plus Reuther and three religious leaders: Rabbi Joaghin Prinz, Matthew

Ahman of the National Catholic Conference for International Justice, and Dr. Eugene Carson Blake, the Presbyterian leader who later became head of the World Council of Churches. Dr. Blake is now retired and living in Connecticut. Godfrey Hodgeson, world renowned author and publisher, caught him in a noisy coffee shop in the Sixth Avenue Hotel; he was described by Hodgeson as being "remarkably out of place." A tall, dignified man who looked like the headmaster of a good private school rather than a civil rights activist, he is still amazed by the chain of events that led to his being on the platform at the march. In June of that year he was caught on a hop by a reporter who asked him just what he proposed to do concretely about civil rights. On the spur of the moment, he committed himself to demonstrate at an amusement park in Baltimore, Maryland, which one of his staff had mentioned just before the press conference. "It was a hilariously successful occasion," he said, "with pictures of Dr. Blake, waving a large hat, entering the paddy wagon, that went all around the world and Robert Spike, Executive Director of the Commission on Religion and Race of the World Council of Churches, parlayed that into getting the churches invited." But before that, the most ticklish event of all had come up. What was the Kennedy administration's attitude going to be?: ". . . Many of our white brothers, as evidenced by their presence here today, have come to realize that their destiny is tied up with our destiny." It is no secret, says Harold Fleming, who is president of the Potomac Institute and was one of the most respected white strategists at the time: "The administration was eager to do anything it could to abort the whole enterprise. It was a welcome event. But when they saw it inevitable, they accommodated to it—or co-opted it depending on how you see it."

"The minute the march was announced," Bayard Rustin recalled, Mr. Randolph began to get calls from the White House, essentially urging that the March not take place. But on June 22, just after the Administration's Civil Rights Bill had gone up on the Hill, some thirty civil rights leaders went to the White House to see the President and discuss the March.

Kennedy's argument was logical, from his point of view; Rusting remembers that once he saw that they were going through with the March, he (Kennedy) said to every department of government to cooperate fully with them and give them everything they wanted. Gradually, almost just as Malcolm X had predicted, it was being changed from the March *on* Washington to the March *in* Washington. Originally, it became a matter of lobbying the Administration subtly; it became a matter of helping the Administration by lobbying Congress.

On August 23, 1963, only three months before John F. Kennedy's assassination, one of the largest and most orderly demonstrations took place in the city of Washington, D.C., ever to be recorded in the history of the federal city. Dr. King was the unanimous choice to lead the March. He had recognized our right to do the things that were done that day and said many times, "The Constitution and the courts guarantee us this right, putting it upon the right of the people to criticize, to dissent, to oppose and to join with others in mass opposition, and to do these things effectively. The first amendment of the Constitution grants us the right peaceably to assemble, and to petition the government for a redress of grievances." King also said, "Many blacks would disobey unjust laws or laws which a minority is compelled to observe which are not binding on the majority." He said that those who do it must accept the penalty imposed by the laws. Supreme Court Justice Abe Fortas added, "This is civil disobedience in a great classic tradition." This was the method used in the demonstrations both before and after the Freedom March on Washington. Justice Abe Fortas, in his book titled *Concerning Dissent and Civil Disobedience,* said: "This is the constructive alternative to violence. . . in time of protest, upheaval, frustration, fear, and moral and legal confusion." He explains this alternative as a means of freedom and survival. He carefully outlines the extent of permissible dissent and civil disobedience, as he describes the crucial, creative roles these nonviolent principles must play in today's revolutionary America.

The civil rights revolution in America can never be merely a Negro revolution. Their future hopes and their children's well-being are caught in racial turmoil that engulfs our land and spreads its corrosive influences across the consciences of every continent. America's racial revolution affects every white citizen because the leadership of Western civilization as a whole is under intense challenge in the world today. In a time where Western wealth and military power are of themselves not enough to guarantee the survival of Western leadership, the future hangs on our ability to breathe enough life into the idea of equal justice under law to fire the imaginations of the world's angry masses in order that they may believe our society worthy of respect and perhaps emulation. The eyes of the whole world are upon the racist problem in the United States because of continued distinctions being made between blacks and whites in this country. The maltreatment of blacks because of racial prejudice is a "gut issue" to the people of Latin America and the continents of Asia and Africa. It is the key to this country's future in a world where a couple of billion black, brown, and yellow people have risen up in an explosive revolution determined to cast off political bondage as well as the shackles of poverty.

Illiteracy and illness are the trappings of second-class status. The seriousness of the race problem at home is reflected in our international problems abroad. We still spend too much money trying to buy friendship of foreign nations and to no avail; the recipients of America's gifts are still throwing ink at our embassies and recently have harassed and killed our ambassadors. All around the world we hear, "Yankee, go home!" These same people would probably at least respect us if we were not so hypocritical with all of the talk about brotherhood of man while holding black people in political and economic slavery right here at home.

Chapter XV
Racist Proliferation

The cost of discrimination cannot be calculated in terms of financial value; no nation or government can put a price tag on it. As the old saying goes, "The best things in life are free or beyond price." Man's priceless possessions are priceless because they are endowed by God. The natural order of life, all that is human, all the creatures of the animal world, even the plants, the trees, the soil, the air, and the water of the earth itself—when these fabrics are destroyed or defaced, no man can recreate them.

Those who met their deaths during the civil rights struggles and over the centuries can never be restored. The children who were murdered, too, are lost to us forever. So are the families that have perished in the fires of the ghettos in northern cities; so are the victims of illnesses who have died in the waiting rooms of overcrowded hospitals for lack of prompt medical care.

Nor can any man put a price tag on hunger, want, misery, hopelessness, squalor, and despair. There is not one real estate operator who would accept money to move this family into his own tenement in the ghetto; there are some things men do not do for money, just as there are some things men do for money only when they can do nothing else. No one can pay a mother for her sorrow or a father for his pride. No one can pay a man for having lost his dignity or manhood; no one can pay a child for his having been denied the joys of childhood; no one can make restitution for human suffering and grief.

The United States cannot indemnify the Negro people for

the long centuries during which our forefathers worked in slavery or for the deprivation of a century of third-class citizenship. She is the richest nation in the history of the world, but she is not that rich. Thus any talk of the high cost of hatred must be viewed in the context that the dollar loses; taken in aggregate, they total only one-thousandth of 1 percent of the suffering of one Negro child in one Atlanta slum for one day, if that.

Even so, the cost of the nation for segregation and discrimination is staggering—running into billions of dollars every month and also radiating out into areas in which many people do not even expect to find Jim Crow. For instance, more white Americans do not link the rapid spread of blight and decay of our central cities to racism, but it is the main cause. Our cities today are taxed beyond their capabilities to provide essential housekeeping services, police and fire protection, garbage collection, and the like, because the white middle class is fleeing from the black.

Taxpayers best able to support essential services have abandoned our cities to those least able to support them, even though the white middle class was also "subsidized" for a time, by the generation that came before it.

Today our big cities are in decline not only because they are aging but because their source of taxing the very tax base that provides for their upkeep is being eroded by the corrosive sublimate of the white man's hatred and the white man's fears. The white man creates the ghettos, brutalizes and exploits the people who inhabit them, and flees from them because of fear. He built Harlem. He creates second-class schools, then fears for his children, lest they be compelled to attend them. He denies Negroes jobs, then curses them for robbing his stores. He creates a climate of despair, then acts surprised when the protest marchers fill the streets and riots erupt.

Our cities cannot survive until whites and Negroes can learn to live together in them. And I mean together, for unless we can share the same neighborhood community center, parks, schools, playgrounds, and stores, the current pattern of segregated living produced by neighborhood transition will go on. And as long as it goes on our cities will continue to decline. I do not know exactly how much our cities are worth, but some have estimated their value at half a trillion dollars. This is just a number to me. But our cities contain the heart of our civilization—the museums and art galleries, cultural institutions, our theaters, libraries, concert halls, civic centers, all that man treasures and prizes. These too are possessions beyond price, and increasingly the white man is denying himself ready access to all that is fine and beautiful in our cultural life by his retreat to suburbia—a retreat from the segregation and blight that he has created.

And to this expense add the cost of building all those superhighways ($1 million per mile) and far-flung subway tunnels to speed the white executive to his downtown office; add to this the cost of creating one hundred little suburban fire chiefs, one hundred little suburban police chiefs, one hundred little suburban tax assessors, and hundred little suburban sewer cleaners, and you begin to get some idea that if segregation costs Negroes, it costs white people, too.

Now I do not mean to say that the suburbs would not have sprung up if Negroes did not move into our cities, but we cannot ignore the proliferation of suburbs, in part because the white man has been running from the black man.

There are some other costs that taxpayers are shelling out, thanks to Jim Crow, and these are better known, but I will mention them anyway. There is the high cost of welfare ($4.3 billion a few years ago), much of it spent in the ghetto. There is the cost of public housing, much of it built in the ghetto, which would be unnecessary if more Negroes could buy their own houses. There is the cost of sending thousands of building inspectors into the field every day to ferret out the violations that the slum landlords produced when they cut up all those single family houses into twelve flats each. There is the cost of arresting, jailing, trying, and paroling all those teenage colored boys for purse-snatching because they cannot find work. There is the cost of all those water shortages—like the ones that affected northern New Jersey and New York City in 1988—in part because slum families don't have a dime to put into the leaky faucet. There is the cost of busing colored children to integrated neighborhoods or schools because so many white families are afraid of integration. Then there is the cost of carrying out all those colored folks from burning buildings when the slums catch fire. And what cities spend on killing rats and roaches, or curing tuberculosis cases, or fixing up sick kids who should not have been sick in the first place, I cannot say, but it must be plenty.

So far, we have discussed only the petty cash items. One of the most sizable costs has been the steady drain on our federal tax dollar to make friends with foreigners was insist on being suspicious of us. We probably shelled out $50 billion in the last three decades for foreign aid trying to win friendship of people—most of them colored—who would love us if only we would just treat their American cousins the way we treat everybody else. And all that "hush money" does not stop them from throwing the worst things they can think of at our embassies and burning down USIA libraries like they did each time an Alabama sheriff hit a woman with a club during the sixties, when billions of dollars started leaving the country injuring our balance of payments. The pain showed on the face of the secretary of treasury as the gold supply dwindled at Fort Knox. President Johnson asked Americans to spend their money on "See America" vacations one year because of our declining gold reserves. That summer, a lot of white people did not get to Paris because of Jim Crow cutting into our gold reserves by clubbing people in Alabama. As usual, black people were not the only ones who took a beating because of racism in the land.

Whitney M. Young, Jr.'s research has found still another big item on the bigotry budget is the cost of underemployment and unemployment. Since white educators do not care much about black children and push them out of school or teach them in third-class schools, not enough of us grow up fit to work in the better technical and professional jobs. So, across the country, a situation has developed where 11.6 percent of all white men are working in such jobs, compared to 4.4 percent of black men.

One consequence of this is that big business today is complaining that it cannot find enough qualified engineers and scientists and administrators at dreadful cost to their operations. Of course, they cannot! Many of the businessmen who cannot find Negro college graduates are sitting on school boards that are doing their best to prevent Negroes from learning anything.

Today Negroes are taking home something over $20 billion a year in wages. Their median yearly family income of $3,233 in only half that of the average white income, which is $5,835. So if Negroes were allowed the same opportunities to work at the same kinds of jobs as white people and to take home the same money, their take-home pay would double to about $40 billion a year.

Phrased another way, this $20 billion we are losing is the equivalent of U.S. exports abroad to all of the 130 nations of the world. Some say that 3 million Americans are employed in their jobs because of trade abroad. Well, by doubling Negro purchasing power you could get the same effect as if you doubled exports and probably put another 3 million men to work!

In the opinion of W. W. Heller, former chairman of the President's Council of Economic Advisors, lifting blacks' income to that of whites would double our current rate of economic growth to 2.5 percent to 5 percent annually.

Compare this with the tax cut, which authorities hope might increase our growth rate by one-half of 1 percent. A survey by the Urban League revealed that if the nonwhite labor force earned as much as their white counterparts, Negroes would spent an additional $3.6 billion on food, $1.7 billion on clothes, $1.5

billion on housing, $1.3 billion on household operations, $1.2 billion on cars and transportation, $5.2 billion on recreation and amusement, $500 million on utilities, and $800 million on personal care and miscellaneous items.

After the beatings of the freedom riders in 1961, capital investment in Birmingham fell off by $67 million in just two years. Snyder M. Myer, president of the Chamber of Commerce in Birmingham, told a Wall Street Journal reporter that big business became convinced, "The state industrial growth will be stunted for months or years" (and since the '64 riots, businessmen in Vulcan City may be talking in terms of decades). If Governor Wallace's appeal for "segregation forever" had gained favor in the North, residents of New York and Chicago would have woken up one morning to read editorials like the one from the Montgomery *Advisor*: "The policy dereliction in Birmingham probably shrank business in every firm in the city. There are a lot of fundamental reasons why city and state cannot use violence in any circumstance. But the most obvious riotous conditions blight profits and payrolls and, politically, make the South's plight worse than it was before."

Another Alabama paper, the Annistan *Star*, editorialized: "Unless we can get more protection from our constituted officers of the law in our cities and countries, we might as well close up our Chamber of Commerce and similar institutions, for no thoughtful person wants to come to a place where both human and property rights are in low repute." Complained one Birmingham resident on this score, "We lost ourselves a generation; they (young people) just do not want to put up with all that racial strife." Birmingham lost not only the flower of its youth, but jobs declined from 246,000 to 228,000 between 1957 and 1963 under the hammer blows of repeated racial outbursts against segregation Wallace style.

Tales of business crippled by racial unrest are legendary, particularly in the South—although Harlem, Philadelphia, and

Patterson, New Jersey, officials can also attest to information supporting that statement. One Jackson, Mississippi, chain store saw sales drop between 40 and 60 percent during 1963's protest. In Charleston, South Carolina, business along thriving King Street fell by as much as 50 percent. New Orleans lost an estimated 4 percent in business when the American Legion shifted its convention to Miami Beach because of lack of decent lodgings for Negro veterans. In the price we pay, according to a recent eye-opening report made by the Southern Regional Council of Atlanta and B'nai B'rith's Anti-Defamation League, the "invisible" cost of hatred appears written on the wall in red ink. This study puts the cost of employment bias alone at $30 billion annually, citing Dr. James Aroy of Atlanta's Emory University Economics Department as its source. Ironically, the loss in personal income hits the southeastern states hardest, he says.

Rep. Charles L. Weltner (Democrat from Georgia) states that Negroes would gain an extra $500 million a year if they were paid the same as whites are.

That is one reason the brightest Negro pupils flock northward as soon as they can get out. In New Orleans, a cockpit of strife over school integration, 750 of the brightest Negro pupils are attending Saint Augustine's School. Their counselor, Fr. Joseph Messina, says that more than 60 percent do not come back.

It is a small wonder personnel officers for Boeing Aircraft and Kaiser Aluminum complain that they cannot find skilled Negro help as in other cities.

And New Orleans is by no means unique. A survey by the *Nashville Tennessean* revealed the state is being drained of 20,000 young people annually—wasting $200 billion tax dollars paid out to school them. One big reason: Jim Crow.

In short, we could fill a telephone book with tales of what cities have lost because of racial hatred. It is important to bear in mind, however, that these losses are not confined to the South. In some ways, the South is moving ahead faster than the North.

In ten years, Atlanta could be way ahead of Pittsburgh, unless sweeping reforms are made. A survey by the National Urban League of 68 cities found that the median income for Negroes fell below $4,000 in twenty-one cities, and among them were northern cities such as Cincinnati, Pittsburgh; Peoria, Springfield, Champion, and Urbana in Illinois; Providence, Rhode Island; and western cities like Phoenix, Wichita, and Tulsa. I point this out to illustrate that not only is suffering and squalor widespread in all our cities, but also to highlight the fact that the depressed condition of the Negro majority is holding back the progress and the prosperity of all their citizens.

White people, particularly trade union officials, must stop looking at Negroes as competitors. We do not just want to compete. We want to contribute. We built the South and we are building today, wherever one turns and looks. But unless more of us get the opportunity to get quality schooling and quality training and quality jobs, we are not going to be using our full potential—and America will be less for it.

So I repeat what I said before. We must march to the libraries as well as to the picket line; we must march to the museums and art galleries and places where we learn as well as in the streets. We must accelerate our fight for qaulity, integrated education, because if we fail in this, we fail in all. Civil rights laws are great. They will speed the end of discrimination in industry. But a law is not going to make any man a nuclear physicist. This we have got to do ourselves.

That is why the Urban League affiliates in seventy-two cities continuously hammer away at the need to keep Johnny in school. That is why the Urban League is mounting job-training programs with federal aid in Cleveland, Buffalo, Pittsburgh, and other cities. That is why we set up national skills banks. Not only do we find qualified people for good jobs but also identify the number of men who do not have such skills and need to be retrained.

I said at the beginning that the nation could never repay

Negroes for what we have suffered. I am convinced of this. But I also believe that for a brief period of time it can mount a national Marshall Plan to help us the way western Europe was helped after World War II. For a time we ought to have families of the poor receiving federal subsidies to boost income to the point where they can break the poverty cycle. Families that can afford books are not going to teach their children to read. Families without food on the table are not going to rear children who are in a condition to learn much in school.

The federal, state, and local governments, private philanthropies, and nonprivate agencies of all kinds will have to team up to help us overcome the centuries of deprivation. If the cost of this is $10 or $20 billion a year, I say pay it. Even in the short run, it will bring a saving for what goes down the financial rat hole due to the high cost of discrimination and segregation. A nation that can afford to put a man on the moon can do as much to help Negro citizens stand on their own feet right here on earth. This is not charity, only fundamental justice, a king of government-issue Bill of Rights for a people who are each day pulling themselves up by their own bootstraps at an ever-increasing speed but who have a long, long way to go.

Chapter XVI
The Question of Race

Benjamin Disraeli in 1880 said no man will treat with indifference the principle of race. It is the key of history, and why history is so often confused is that it was written by men who were ignorant of this principle and all the knowledge it involves. Carl T. Rowan directed the U.S. Information Agency and its many-sided effort to "Sell America" and to explain American actions and principles to the world. This experience gave Rowan the evidence that Disraeli was correct; race is the key to history. Rowan's book, *No Whitewash for U.S. Abroad*, went on to explain: "It is the key to this country's future." He made reference to the Third World one billion strong: black, brown, and yellow people who have risen up to an explosive revolution, determined to cast off political bondage as well as the shackles of poverty, illiteracy, and illness that are the trappings of second-class status.

Race or the question of whether our generations of men have learned enough to surmount the difference of race is also the key to the fateful issue of war and peace.

Rowan said in one of his speeches before an Urban League audience at Howard Univerity in March of 1961, "If you ask me what I would like most to see happen in world affairs today, I would give top priority to a disarmament agreement or a settlement of the Berlin dispute—or any such agreement—to having it demonstrated that, beyond any doubt, a bi-racial or multi-racial society (can live in) harmony or mutual respect. I feel that long after conflict with the West and Soviet Union communism has faded, we shall still be plagued by this issue of race."

Common even before the Sino-Soviet split became evident was talk such as, "In a few years we may have to join the Russians to fight the Chinese." And in 1961, the magnitude of racial feeling in Britain, the depth of the feeling over caste and color in India, and the obvious enmity between Negroes and Arabs in such places as the Sudan all lent support to my convictions that race was an international problem not to be taken lightly. What I have seen in the years since has strengthened my convictions that racial bigotry and bitterness, racial arrogance ingrained over generations, is the ugly and ominous timebomb that spells danger to mankind. What I have seen in four years as a government official has caused me to understand more acutely than ever before the grim fact that the United States' worst critical domestic problem is also one of our most worrisome international problems. That is why the civil rights revolution in America can never be merely a Negro Revolution. Whether white Americans wills it or not, their destiny or futures, their hopes, their children's well-being are caught up in the racial turmoil that engulfs our land and runs its corrosive influences across the consciences of every continent.

This is a revolution that affects every white American, because as President Johnson said in his historic voting rights address before a joint session of Congress, in our time we have experienced grave dangers and the issues of war, peace, prosperity, and oppression are ubiquitous. But seldom at any time does an issue reveal the secret heart of the United States itself. Nor are we met with a challenge, contrary to our growth or abundance, or our welfare or our security, but rather to the values and the purposes and the meaning of our beloved nation. The equal rights issues for black Americans is such an issue. Should the United States defeat every enemy and conquer the stars and yet remain unequal in this issue, then we will have failed as a people and a nation.

America's racial revolution is a product of hatred that has smoldered in this land because of bigotry in the hearts of men in places of power who were not man enough to stand up and be counted to rid our country of the cancerous sore of racism. The right of every American to first-class citizenship is the most important issue of our times. That is why we of black ancestry fight for that right. We have no illusions about the difficulties that lie ahead. We know that bigots intend to go on fighting us and will continue to use the big lie that blacks are inferior based solely on skin color. We know that no matter how far we progress, the lie will still be there. We know that this lie must be exposed and destroyed if the United States is to survive. We know our stake in the United States is great and the future is bright for black children as well as white. That is why we continue to fight:

We have paid a hard price throughout the world in current years for the outbreaks of racial conflicts in our country. There are remote areas of the world where Little Rock and Selma are more familiar names than Chicago or Washington, D.C., and for the simple reason that the first two cities have been the focus of highly publicized events that were "gut issues" to the dark inhabitants of these remote areas.

At the time of the Birmingham violence, Carl T. Rowan was doing this tenure as ambassador to Finland, and he wrote: "My tenure was one of delights and pleasures, but there was one routine that I dreaded: getting up morning after morning to find half a dozen newspapers full of headlines and photographs of racial violence in Birmingham, of police dogs, fire hoses, mass arrests and assorted commentaries about police barbarity."

Finnish newspapers were sharp in their denunciation of America's shame, and I soon discovered that no plantation, however logical, was a match for the seering emotional impact of one particularly offensive photograph: that of a policeman holding a Negro woman to the ground by pressing his knee to her throat.

Seeing the angry and damaging reaction among the fair-haired, blue-eyed Nordics of Scandinavia, I scarcely had to guess what the reaction was among the colored peoples of the world.

I later saw some samples. "Billions of U.S. dollars spent for aid and propaganda are useless when the world hears of this preposterous discrimination," said a newspaper in Cairo.

The generally friendly Nigeria, in the *Morning Post* stated that "President Kennedy had to be feeling quite small, not only in the eyes of the Soviets, who have never believed the Americans anyway, but in the eyes of the world, to whom he was always represented his country as the champion of Liberty." As the editorial said, "The brutes of Alabama, after all, knocked the bottom out of all these preachments about the free world, America is building herself up as the most barbarian state in the world." The best that could be said of us in Africa that season was said in Ethiopia, when a daily paper admitted "at least the U.S. in not hiding anything."

It was the sending of federal troops to Alabama that changed the headlines from the violence and jailings: "U.S. Troops in Alabama" headlined the Nigerian press. "Kennedy does it fine!"

In response to the passage of the Civil Rights Bill, Nigeria's *Daily Telegraph* wrote: "The American people have shown in strong terms that when the choice is between honor and infamy, they will choose the cause of honor, the only one worthy of those who claim they hold the key to democracy."

The East African Standard commented that "endorsement by the bill must have been welcomed with relief not only by the majority of the Americans at home, but also by those whose job it is to project American policies and influences abroad."

Along with explaining to the world such things as our policies in Vietnam, the Dominican Republic, Berlin, and elsewhere, it fell to my lot sixteen months ago to direct USIA's effort to create a better worldwide understanding of race relations in the United States. Our task has been not to whitewash the situation, for it is obvious that the incidents of racial discrimination in our open society could not be hidden, no matter how desperately some Americans might want them hidden. So what we have done is present an honest picture of United States struggling as no society ever struggled to erase these insidious discriminations based on such incidental facts as race, color, national origin, and religion. We have tried to have the world understand that the story of racial development in the United States is not simply a story of Klansmen, church bombings and murder on our highways, but also many tender, inspiring stories of great physical and moral courage on the part of Americans, both black and white.

The one thing that has been constantly obvious is that this is one job USIA cannot do with any Madison Avenue hocus pocus. In no area of our endeavors is time more evident than in this field of race relations. Through our media we can project the American image, but we cannot create it. Here it is the businessman in Chicago, the school board chairmen in Houston, or the pool hall loiterer in Podunk who has the capacity to say and do the things that make for a good or bad image.

Fortunately, the federal government is also a strong force in this area and in the last several years has played a most constructive role. I recall that in 1963 one Cairo newspaper noted that "Enlightened elements in the USA are taking the leadership of President Kennedy and his Administration, a position that reveals this understanding of general developments, the direction of world currents and U.S. interests."

Another Middle Eastern newspaper, praising the role of the U.S. government in ensuring that James Meredith would be permitted to stay at the University of Mississippi, asked: "Is there any other state that would spend $5 million to enable one of its citizens to obtain his rights?"

The same identity of colored people abroad with the American Negro's fate was expressed in the aftermath of Selma's tragic events, and the reputation of the United States rose perhaps to its highest point.

Said the *Free Press Journal* of Bombay: "Selma may well go down in American history as the last great barrier to civilization and freedom in the United States."

"The government is doing its best to make all Americans

equal before the law, and the freedom fighters are winning the battle by non-violent means," said the Ethiopian *Herald*. "President Johnson is leading the Negro revolution from the top. Martin Luther King is leading from below. White Americans have joined hands with their Negro brothers in protest marches . . . victory is in sight and the 'Great Society' is being insured for a better tomorrow."

Tunisia's *Petit Matin* described the federal government's application of the civil rights law as "an expression of the will of the American People." The Tanganyika *Standard* incorporated in an editorial: "Dr. King's description of the President's voting rights speech at one of the most eloquent, unequivocal, and passionate pleas for human rights ever made by a president of the United States."

The American people must be forthright and courageous in responding to this leadership from the government. A president can make a declaration of integrity for his country, but only with the citizens of that country can he infuse the declaration with the substance of life, man's future, not twenty years from now, but as far as ahead as men of great vision dare look. Success may be determined in large measure by whether or not the American people meet these new principles of race or, as Disraeli warned against, whether they treat them lightly.

Chapter XVII
The Classic March for Freedom

On the day of the Freedom March, 250,000 people, both black and white, some children of ex-slaves, American Indians, and sympathizers, along with other ethnic groups, met to voice their grievances at the place fashioned after the Parthenia on the Acropolis in Greece. Inside is the awe-inspiring statue of Abraham Lincoln, our sixteenth president of the United States. It took Daniel Chester French four years and twenty-eight blocks of white marble to carve the nineteen-foot statue. The planners of the march could not have picked a more appropriate place. Crowds of people sat clustered together at the reflecting pool just in front of the Lincoln Memorial. Some soaked their feet in the water; others sat quietly on the grass, and not one unkind word was spoken as the crowd grew bigger and bigger. There were thousands of extra police called on duty, fearing the worst outbreak of violence ever. But the police were disappointed to find only traffic to direct. Personally, I got only as far as the corner of Fifteenth and Constitution Avenue, N.W., where I was allowed to discharge my passengers, who, prior to my picking them up, had come twenty miles on foot; for fear of missing the speeches, they had hailed my cab and asked to be taken as close as I could take them to the focal point. History was in the minds and muscles of the people on that memorable day.

Earlier that day, thousands had gathered at the Washington Monument for an orderly march down Constitution and Independence avenues to the Lincoln Memorial. There were relaxed and uplifted faces singing "We Shall Overcome." Signs bobbed up and down that read: *EFFECTIVE CIVIL RIGHTS LAWS NOW; INTEGRATED SCHOOLS NOW; DECENT HOUSING NOW.* As they reached the Lincoln Memorial and settled themselves on the grass, the program commenced.

I thought in retrospect that the architect Henry Bacon, who fashioned the Lincoln Memorial three decades before the march, had designed a place suitable for the occasion. The exact spot where the memorial is now located was chosen while it was still beneath the Potomac River. As a matter of fact, six hundred acres of East Potomac Park were drained and reclaimed to make the construction of the Lincoln and Jefferson memorials possible. So one century after the signing of the Emancipation Proclamation, the place chosen for the great emancipator's statue had become a showplace—a suitable backdrop for the Rev. Dr. Martin Luther King, Jr., and the other speakers to call for a reality of the American dream for at least 25 million black Americans who were yet outside of the democratic way of life, right here in the United States of America.

The march had brought people from all parts of the country. Many came from far across the seas—they came by plane, by car, by bus, by train, and they came walking, cycling, and even hitchhiking—but they came. They came to sing, to shout their cry for freedom, and they came to listen. And for almost three hours they listened to a multitude of speakers who demanded passage of a civil rights bill, providing the basic guarantees of the Constitution. Washington, D.C. has been the site for myriads of celebrations, with much flag waving and cheering crowds here in this city of the nation's capital. We have celebrated kings and queens of foreign nations, inaugurated presidents, welcomed home triumphant warriors to celebrate their victories. Following the end of the Civil War, people paraded for two days and two nights down Pennsylvania Avenue, N.W. In all of this I have found no parallel in terms of greatness to the 1963 Civil Rights March, which took place the year that marked the one hundreth anniversary of the signing of the Emancipation Proclamation. This is gradualism.

On August 28, 1963, they listened to a man who summed up for all the previous speakers the objectives of the march. Dr. King, having weighed the total situation, spoke as a Baptist minister that day, communicating in a way that God enables His ministers to do when they are speaking on behalf of righteousness, justice, and truth: "Who maketh His angels spirits; and His ministers a flaming fire." He struck a cord of sympathy with people who believe in Christ the world over. There, at the Memorial of Lincoln, was an awe-inspiring fervor pervading the atmosphere as Dr. King delivered a "down home" gospel message. The spirit of God moved as Dr. King, in his deep baritone voice, exploited the legacy. It was late afternoon when he took his place at the lectern and spoke the following words:

> One hundred and five years ago, a great American, in whose symbolic shadow we stand, signed the Emancipation Proclamation. This decree came as a great beacon light to millions of Negro slaves who had been seared in the flames of withering injustice. It came as a joyous daybreak to end the long night of captivity, but one hundred years later we must face the fact that the Negro still is not free. One hundred years later . . . the life of the Negro is still crippled by the manacles of segregation and the chains of discrimination. One hundred years later, the Negro is still languishing in a corner of American society and finds himself an exile in his own land. So we have come here today to dramatize an appalling condition. In a sense we have come to our nation's capital to cash a check. When the architects of our Republic wrote the magnificent words of the Constitution and the Declaration of Independence, they were signing the inalienable rights of life, liberty and the pursuit of happiness.
>
> It is obvious today that America has defaulted on this promissory note insofar as her citizens of color are concerned. Instead of honoring this sacred obligation, America has given the Negro people a check which has come back marked "insufficient funds."

But we refuse to believe that there are insufficient funds in the great vaults of opportunity of this nation. So we have come to cash this check, a check that will give us upon demand, the riches of freedom and the security of justice. We have also come to this hallowed spot to remind America of the fierce urgency of now. This is no time to engage in the luxury of cooling off or to take the tranquilizing drug of gradualism. Now is the time to make real the promises of democracy. Now is the time to arise from the dark and the desolate valley of segregation to the sunlit path of radical justice. Now is the time to open the doors of opportunity to all God's children. Now is the time to lift our nation from the quicksands of injustice to the solid rock of brotherhood.

It would be fatal for the nation to overlook the urgency of the moment and to understand the determination of the Negro. This sweltering summer of the Negro's legitimate discontent will not pass until there is an invigorating autumn of freedom and equality. Nineteen Hundred and Sixty-Three is not an end but a beginning; those who hoped that the Negro needed to blow off steam and will now be content will have a crude awakening if the nation returns to business as usual. There will be neither rest nor tranquility in America unless he is granted his citizenship rights. The whirlwinds of revolt will continue to shake the foundations of our nation until the bright day of justice emerges.

But there is something that I must say to my people who stand on the warm threshold which leads into the palace of justice. In the process of gaining our rightful places we must not be guilty of wrongful deeds. Let us not seek to satisfy our thirst for freedom by drinking from the cup of bitterness and hatred. We must forever conduct our struggle in the high plane of dignity and discipline. We must not allow our creative protest to degenerate in physical violence. Again and again we must rise to the majestic height of meeting physical force with soul force. The marvelous new militance which has engulfed the Negro community must not lead us to distrust all white people, for many of our white brothers as evidenced by their presence here today have come to realize that their destiny is tied up with our destiny. And their freedom is tied up with our freedom. We cannot walk alone.

And as we walk we must make the pledge that we shall march ahead. We cannot turn back. There are those who are asking the devotees of civil rights, "When will you be satisfied?" We can never be satisfied as long as the Negro is the victim of unspeakable horrors of police brutality. We can never be satisfied as long as our bodies, heavy with the fatigue of travel, cannot gain lodging in the motels of the highways and hotels of the cities. We cannot be satisfied as long as the Negro's basic mobility is from a smaller ghetto to a large one. We cannot be satisfied as long as a Negro in Mississippi cannot vote and a Negro in New York believes he has nothing for which to vote. No, we are not satisfied, and we will not be satisfied until justice rolls down like water and righteousness like a mighty stream.

I am not unmindful that some of you have come here out of great trials and tribulations. Some of you have come from narrow jail cells. Some of you have come from areas where your quest for freedom left you battered by the storms of persecution and staggered by the winds of police brutality. You have been the veterans of creating. Continue to work with the faith that unearned suffering is redemptive.

Go back to Mississippi. Go back to Louisiana. Go back to South Carolina. Go back to Georgia. Go back to the ghettos and slums of our northern cities knowing that somehow this situation can and will be changed. Let us not wallow in the valley of despair. I say to you today, my friends, that in spite of the difficulties and frustrations of the moment I still have a dream. It is a dream deeply rooted within the American dream. I have a dream that one day this nation will rise up and live out the true meaning of its creed: "We hold these truths to be self-evident that all men are created equal."

I have a dream that one day on the red hills of Georgia, the sons of former slaves and sons of former slaveholders will be able to sit down at the table of brotherhood together. I have a dream that one day even the state of Mississippi, a desert state, sweltering with the heat of injustice and oppression, will be transformed into an oasis of freedom and justice. I have a dream that my four children will one day live in a nation where they will be judged by the content of their character, not the color of their skin. I have a dream today. I have a dream that one day in the State of Alabama, whose governor's lips are presently dripping with the words of interposition and nullification, will be transformed into a situation where little black boys will be able to join hands with little white boys and little white girls and will walk together as sisters and brothers. I have a dream today.

I have a dream that one day every valley shall be exalted. Every hill and mountain shall be made low. The rough places will be made plains and the crooked places will be made straight, and the glory of the Lord shall be revealed, and all flesh shall see it together.

This is the hope. This is the faith with which I return to the South. With this faith we will be able to hew out of the mountain a stone of hope. With this faith we will be able to transform the jangling discords of our nation into a beautiful symphony of brotherhood. With this faith we will be able to work together, to pray together, to struggle together, to go to jail together, to stand up for freedom together, knowing that we will be free one day. This will be the day when all of God's children will be able to sing together with new meaning. "My country 'tis of thee, sweet land of liberty, of thee I sing. Land of the Pilgrims' pride, land where my fathers died. From every mountainside, let freedom ring." And if America is to be a great nation this must become true. So let freedom ring from the prodigious hilltops of New Hampshire. Let freedom ring from the mighty mountains of New York. Let freedom ring from the heightening Alleghenies of Pennsylvania! Let freedom ring from the snow-capped Rockies of Colorado. Let freedom ring from the curvaceous peaks of California! But not only that. Let freedom ring from every hill and every molehill of Mississippi. From every mountainside let freedom ring. When we let freedom ring from every village and hamlet, from every state and every city, we will be able to speed up that day when all God's children, black men and white men, Jews and Gentiles, Protestants and Catholics, will be able to join hands and sing in the words of that old Negro spiritual: "Free at last! Free at last! Thank God almighty, we are free at last!"

When the benediction was announced and the crowd dispersed, most walked away in faith that there would be a very definite change from that point forward. The event turned out to be one of the most well-conducted marches ever staged in the city of Washington, D.C., maybe because so many there were affected by the outcome.

Chapter XVIII
Social Change

That day was the destruction of a stereotype. That was no shiftless, irresponsible, ineducable race that brought off the march on Washington. That stereotype was the excuse used for three centuries to continue the oppression of black Americans. Since the march, one is not easily tempted to believe the "factual lies of oppression." The black history of this country tell us, as opposed to the lies of oppression, that no one in this country has done more work than black people. As a matter of fact, there is a historical account log and list of accomplishments that tells us that we are not what white media say we are. Black history repudiates that history aptly called by blacks "lies agreed upon." Because of the germinal insights of Carter Woodson, W. E. Du Bois, William Lee Hansberry, Benjamin Quarles, John Hope Franklin, C. L. R. James, Vincent Harding, Mary Berry, John Henrick Clark, John Blassingame, and Charles Vessy, to name only a few, we have been able to chart our course based on truth.

The March on Washington was a mobilization of the latent energy in the masses. This must continue in spirit if we are to make ourselves available to ourselves and to history. To quote Lerone Bennett, "We must make history available to all levels." The march was a prime example of "getting scholarly materials out of the libraries and books into the minds and muscles of the people." The year 1960 began a revival of black history that put pressure on boards of education and the white media. This pressure must continue if that old demon of racial prejudice is to be bound.

Also, as Mr. Bennett has suggested, "Black organizations, including churches, should organize adult education classes, study groups and forums. There is also a need for the publication of popular pamphlets on the issues and personalities of black history."

This issue is crucial because the history of the people is not worth the paper it is written on if it is not concretized. White history commands attention today because white history is concretized in the buildings we use, the streets we walk, the holidays we celebrate, the institutions we serve. If black history is to become meaningful, it must become equally concrete and equally alive. We must understand the past; we must project it in popular forms, but we must also assume the burden of the past in action. The whole swirling history of black Americans is capsulized today by the struggles in the streets of the United States. One understands that by relating oneself creatively to that struggle and by assuming one's obligations to history, in the final analysis, one reads history in order to learn how to make history. And one makes history not by reading, not by debating, not by resolving, but by acting in such a way as to deserve a certain past. We do not, as is commonly supposed, receive a past. We make it by resuming the past in a contemporary project based on projection into the future. In other words, we give the past a meaning by acting in the present. A truly married man, for example, gives meaning to that vow he made ten years ago by acting today in a manner that gives meaning to that vow. By the same token, racism maintains the original product of American slavery by projects that give contemporary meaning to slavery. Similarly, blacks give meaning to the strivings of Dr. Martin King, Jr., Malcolm X, and Frederick Douglass by what they do today.

Excellence in art, music, and sports is the heritage bequeathed to Afro-America so that we might gain freedom and fame to rise above the shackles that once held us fast. The black athlete's story is secured in American history by the young stars who are up and coming and headed for the record books. Some black athletes who have achieved fame are: Isaac Murphy, the greatest and the most immortal black jockey, who won the Kentucky Derby three times; Jack Johnson, the first black heavyweight champion and perhaps the greatest fighter of all times; Josh Gibson, "the greatest right-hand hitter of all time," immortal black catcher for the Homestead Grays; Muhammad "I Am the Greatest" Ali, the irrepressible poet and champion who told the world that he was the greatest and went on to prove it; Marion Motley, the first black player to enter Football's Hall of Fame; Wilma Rudolph, the polio victim who went on to become the greatest women runner in America's history; Jesse Owens, the incredible track star who won four gold medals in the Olympics; Charlie Sifford, the first black man to win a professional golf tournament; and Kareem Abdul Jabbar (formerly Lew Alcindor), the towering basketball star who is the greatest superstar of all.

Almost thirty years ago, Branch Rickey broke the seemingly impenetrable color line of organized baseball by bringing in Jackie Robinson. He will never be forgotten by the millions of sports fans who cheer heroes. Jackie Robinson's words, following the results, became an immortal response for Afro-Americans in the continuing struggle. The fight against bigotry and discrimination in sports is no different from the fight for freedom being waged by all blacks. Jackie Robinson's acceptance speech could have been my own. Jackie Robinson said the following: "All I ask is that you respect me as a human being. I am proud to be a black. I am not ashamed of my dark skin. God has given us certain unique qualities and we cherish them just as Englishmen, Frenchmen, Jews, Indians, and every other group of common origin cherish theirs."

As early as the 1700s, not long after the first shiploads of blacks had arrived from West Africa, the colonists began racing horses. The early American colonist, equipped with horses, men, and the time, turned to racing Thoroughbreds. They turned over the job of training them to their slaves, and the blacks became so knowledgeable in the peculiar ways of Thoroughbreds that black jockeys and trainers became the toast of the American turf world.

Racing began in England, dating back to the twelfth century. The new Americans, who looked for diversions from the rigors of everyday life, picked races that were match affairs, with heavy wagering between owners and partisans of sectional favorites. Descriptions of some of the matches and the names of the jockeys, like Pompey, Scipio, Cato, and Caesar, illustrate that it was customary among slaveowners of that period to air their knowledge of the classics by bestowing the names of the great Romans upon their chattels.

These types of matches held sway until the start of the Civil War. There were attempts to set up organized racing in Virginia, Maryland, and Kentucky, but the first Thoroughbred racing meet in the country was held at the Saratoga Springs, New York, track in 1863. Belmont Park in Long Island, New York, opened three years later. Black jockeys, experts by now in training and riding, came along. One black rider on record was known only as Abe. In the Inaugural Jerome Handicap at Belmont he won with a horse named "Watson," and he won again at the first Travers Stakes at Saratoga with Merrill.

Churchill Downs at Louisville, Kentucky, opened its track in 1875, and the first Kentucky Derby was held that year. Of the fifteen jockeys riding in that first Kentucky Derby, fourteen were blacks, but their names did not appear on the program. One of the blacks, Oliver Lewis, stepped down with the winner Aristotle. The distance was a mile and one-half, instead of the mile and one-quarter of today, with a time of 2:37 3/4, the fastest time ever run by a three-year-old in the United States until then. Today the world record for that distance is 2:26.

Jack Orr's book, titled *The Black Athlete: His Story in American History*, shows that other black trainers and jockeys made their mark in this beginning period. Trainer James Williams saddled the 1876 Derby winner Vagrant Trainer. Jockey Ed Brown saddled Brown Dick. Brown and jockey Billy Walker won the next year with Baden-Baden. Walker was also up on Broeck when he won by ten lengths a two-mile match race against a California mare, Molly McCarthy. Garrison Lewis won the 1880 Derby; Babe Hurd won the classic in 1882. A former jockey, Raleigh Colston, trained Leonatus, winner in 1883.

But the outstanding rider of the period was the Afro-American Isaac Murphy. He achieved immortality by winning three Kentucky Derbies, a record that stood for forty years, until tied by Earl Sands in 1930. Later the record was beaten by Eddie Arcaro, who won five Derbies (1938, 1941, 1945, 1948, and 1952). In this generation, Bill Hartack won four, and Willie Shoemaker has three to his credit.*

---

*Jack Orr, *The Black Athlete: His Story in American History* (Scarsdale, New York: Lion Books, 1969).

Chapter XIX
Aspiration to Black Unity

To all black Americans Dr. Martin Luther King has shown the way in which we must travel and persist to travel that history may record our progress, for truth is marching on. Men, like ships, become derelicts on the sea of life if they are without direction, and we were at a point and a time in history where out of necessity there must be a moving of the black spirit. True, we were heading in the right direction, but at the same time we were going backward or drifting to the side of our mark in society. There were, as before stated, many black leaders of civil rights demonstrations, but Dr. King emerged at the forefront of the battle to consolidate the leadership of the black movement.

The Bible declares that without a vision, the people perish (Proverbs 29:18). Dr. King was a man with a vision. I find the other part of the verse quoted from the Book of Proverbs equally important: "But he that keepeth the law, happy is he." Both portions of the Scripture describe the men who faced violence with nonviolence and won.

One understands history in sum by participation in action that is carrying that history to an unknown fulfillment. A person understands the history I have been talking about when she understands that she is a wave in a historical current that has flowed through the ages and is flowing now, taking her, whether she wills it or not, to a shore shrouded in mist.

A person understands history when he understands that history does not permit men the luxury of escaping their inheritance, when he understands that he is not only responsible for his own acts but also for the meanings those acts take on in a certain social context, when he understands that he is not only what he has done but what his parents have done, when he understands that history requires him to answer not only for his own life but also for the lives of the men and women and children who share his situation and his destiny.

It is on this deep level, and within the context of concrete responsibilities, that black history assumes its true meaning. And if we situate ourselves on that level and allow our history to free the power that is within us, as Lerone Bennett says, we will become a people, once lost to history, who awakened to themselves and transformed history.

Dr. King was as necessary as the calendar and the clock to the building blocks of black history. Without a standard of measure in the realm of time, one would be lost in the great expanse of our universe; without the acceptance or knowledge of the compass, one would be lost and could never find his way; without the acceptance of the facts of distance and direction, one could not locate oneself as to one's position upon life's way. Had not Bayard Rustin and A. Philip Randolph, the leaders of the march, in their planning recognized and agreed that it was time for a new massive front in order to bring home to the people that the struggle was moving into a new phase, they might never have chosen Dr. King, who was in every respect right for the job of leading the march. Why? Because he could articulate the needs and demands of second-class citizens, who through no fault of their own had not yet fully covered the bet that had been placed, which must be covered today. It is easy to see from Dr. King's activities and the books he wrote, especially *Why We Can't Wait*, that he understood that the time was right to answer for black Americans' web of relationships into which we were born and for which we must now answer. Even we see that he possessed the knowledge and ability to narrate the past activities of black history and cause us to prepare for action.

John H. Johnson, editor and publisher of *Jet* and *Ebony* magazines, stated in a special issue of *Ebony* in August 1984 that the road to freedom for black America is black politics; these magazines have, from my childhood, served as counselors on black history to millions of black Americans like myself, and I have found it almost impossible to write on such a topic without quoting members of the Johnson Publishing Company and its staff. Lerone Bennett, Jr., journalist, historian, and senior editor of *Ebony* magazine, has through the years relayed a learning experience to Afro-America and the world. I feel that it is only appropriate that the people who have kept the record and done research for forty years or more show the progress and the economic gains of a people who started with nothing but a song and faith, which "is the substance of things hoped for, the evidence of things not seen" (Hebrews 11:1).

Life with all its heartaches, failures, and accomplishments
Appears like a vapor; then soon it is spent

We set our goals in life, and through blood, sweat, and tears, we
work hard to achieve them,
and all through the years we aspire to make our ascent.

William Shakespeare best describes man in saying,
the world is a stage and upon it we're playing;
as the human drama goes on.

Alexander died in 323 B.C. before completing his plan for world unity. He conquered most of the then known world and created
a world state.
Historians observed that even today
man experiences a life forlorn.

How can the people live together in peace
in a world so filled with frustration?

How can the void of so many nations be filled
With freedom and justification?

The empires of Julius Caesar, Alexander the Great,
and my own, said Napoleon while reminiscing,
were built upon force, greed, and hate but today
they are all gone; they are nonexisting.

Then came Jesus of whom the prophets spoke,
The Prince of Peace; the humble Nazarene
Seeking to change man's heart, he built upon love,
He gave gifts unto men and has risen above.
Fiery evangelist, orators, and heroes were changed
From a stockpile of ignorant fisherman.

Segregation laws in the United States prevailed until 1954,
when the Supreme Court decided it to be no more,
In so doing fate threw open the door
for the Afro-American quest for freedom to soar.

We arrived here laden with chains,
And our bodies were racked with pain.
Plain to see we were brought for one purpose.
For the great white father's aim, to usurp us.

There was no plan for the slaves' "advancement"
Only devised scheme for subservient enhancement.
In the process of becoming rich in this nation
Blacks were corralled on the masters' plantation.

We were property, like cattle fit into the equation
And forced to serve the Caucasian persuasion.
But this country has undergone the evolution
That caused us to amend our constitution.

According to the Scripture we have all gone astray.
We have turned, every one of us, to his own way,
But God has laid upon Christ the iniquities of us all.
If we trust in Him He'll never let us fall.

America has become a refuge for all people,
For the exile, the outcast, the adroit, and the feeble.
We must all stand together for justice with bold bravery
And resist any cause that means contemporary slavery.

In this vein, Anthony Benezet, the eighteenth-century emancipator,
To Martin Luther King, our contemporary arbitrator
Continues the dialogue of civil rights until King's demise,
Then passes on the baton and as his spirit filled the skies:
"Free at last, free at last!" we still hear his cries.

—Cecil Thompson, Sr.

Victor Hugo, poet, dramatist, and novelist and perhaps the most important of the French Romantic writers, spoke the proverbial words: "Nothing, neither an army nor legislation, nor an armed sheriff, can withstand the strength of an idea whose time has come." Likewise, when I as an Afro-American representative look back at the road upon which I have trod and look at the signs of the time, I, like Victor Hugo and with the same visionary poetry, must say that "our time has come."

The coming of the new political time as announced by the sharp increases in black voter registration and participation, the election of black mayors in Chicago and Philadelphia, and the Jesse Jackson presidential campaign brought about the shift in political sensibility of black Americans, who exploded in the years 1983 and 1984 in the most intense political fever since the first reconstruction period one hundred years ago. The sleeping giant that awakened in the 1980s has pushed black and white

America across a critical threshold and in this last decade of the 1990s established Governor Wilder of Virginia and Mayor Dinkins of New York City, New York, in places of power only dreamed of by black people a few short years ago.

Between 1970 and 1980, according to the Bureau of the Census, the power of black numbers has increased by 17.3 percent, from 22.6 million to 26.5 million by 1980, and blacks constituted more than 20 percent of the population in seven states: Mississippi (35 percent), South Carolina (30 percent), Louisiana (29 percent), Georgia (27 percent), Alabama (26 percent), Maryland (23 percent), and North Carolina (22 percent). No less telling was the power of black numbers at the municipal level: New York City (25.2 percent), Chicago (39.8 percent), Philadelphia (37.8 percent), Atlanta (66.6 percent), Detroit (63.1 percent), New Orleans (55.3 percent), and Washington, D.C. (70.3 percent). These facts indicate that our faith has become sight and produced the fundamental miracle of showing Afro-Americans where we must go from here.

It is unmistakably clear from all this that an increasing number of black Americans have decided that politics is the new road to freedom. Is this a new vision or an old illusion? Can the new politics deliver the goods and services and jobs that are the meaning and the end of politics? That is the central question, for the fundamental problem of politics is translation of votes into political power and the translation of political power into economic and cultural power. Somebody said once that "politics is the science of who gets what, where, when and how much." Can the new politics deliver on that level?

The answer to this question, according to experts quoted in this issue, is that politics is a way, perhaps the only way, and there is no alternative to using the only major weapon in our hands. The available evidence supports this view, according to the JCPS. Black employment in city government, 1973–80, shows a strong correlation between black political influence and the number and quality of municipal jobs held by blacks in forty cities. There is also evidence that black political power has increased services to black communities and stimulated black business development.

This is the harvest of the first stage of the new political time, and the challenge before black voters and black politicians is the total mobilization of black voting power for major breakthroughs on the economic and cultural levels. Whether the coming of our time becomes a new time and a new direction for the United States depends on the responses of all Americans to unprecedented hopes and challenges presented in the following.

The Congressional Black Caucus is fast becoming one of the main attractions for limousines in Washington, D.C. In addition, the Bankers Convention, which as a rule uses every available limousine in town, lately has competition from our team on Capitol Hill, who for the past fourteen years have begun to do exploits, and more and more limousines are being used to transport people to gala festivities; it is one of the annual events that generates excitement in Washington, D.C.

As a tour guide in the nation's capital, where more than 15 million people from the United States and around the world pass through each year, I have found it a great joy and a privilege for me to greet some of them. For the last several years I have been located on the Ellipse, just in the rear of the White House, selling tours to people who might otherwise take the Tourmobile.

In addition to the English language, I have been blessed with the ability to speak and write Spanish, French, and Italian fluently, which I do while showing people around our national monuments. Most tourists who set out for a day of sightseeing almost always are attracted to the Ellipse, where the information booths for Tourmobile seek to usurp authority over all competitors who serve in the same capacity. They spread their literature with free coupons in all the hotels, which makes it appear as though they are the only legitimate means of sightseeing transportation in Washington. In reality, there are about thirty or forty old professionals left who are determined to give better tours, but in order to do so, we must position ourselves in juxtaposition on the sidewalk near the booth and speak to as many people as we can about the tour we have to offer—it is always better to communicate in their native tongue.

French Dialogue

Guide: Bon jour. . .comment allez-vous aujourdui? Je suis un quide pour touristes. Que voulez vous voir les endroit historique? Je p'eur vous montre le ville: le Capitol, dè les Etats Uni la Maison Blanche, y le Cemetair d'Arlington, La Tombe de Soldat Inconnu et le Batiment, d'Histoire Naturelle.

Client: Mais oui, nous sommes ici a faire cela; nous vien d'arriver, ma femme et moi.

Guide: Soyez le bienvenue. Be welcome.

Client: Vous avez un tres bon accent.

Guide: Merci beaucoup.

Client: Je vous en prie Monsieur. . . .Allons y. J'ai envie de partir.

Guide: D'accord.

English Translation

Guide: Good morning. . .How are you today? I am a tour guide for the city. Would you like to see the national monuments? I can show you all the important places of historical value: the Capitol, the White House, and Arlington Cemetery, where the Changing of the Guards takes place at the Tomb of the Unknown Soldier. We'll end up at the Natural History Building.

Client: We have just arrived, my wife and I, but this is exactly what we want.

Guide: Welcome.
Client: You have a very good accent.
Guide: Thank you.
Client: You're welcome, sir. . . . Let's go. I feel like leaving.
Guide: Agreed. Let's go.

Italian Dialogue

Guide: Bon Giorno, come sta lei stamatina? Per favore dove piacerebbe andare? Washington et una citta famosa. Ci sono molti palazzi bellissimi.
Client: Puo guardare tutti? . . . posso lei portare addesso al museo de art, Cominciamo.
Guide: Le piacerebbe?
Client: Si mi piacerebbe? Cuanto vale questo?
Guide: Venticinque dolares. D'accordo. Ecco la recevuta.
Client: Molte grazia.
Guide: Niente affatto.

English Translation

Guide: Good morning. How are you this morning? Where would you like to go, may I ask? Washington is a world famous city with many beautiful buildings.
Client: Can I see everything?
Guide: I can take you now; we'll begin at the art museum. Would you like to go?
Client: Yes, I would. How much does it cost?
Guide: Twenty-five dollars.
Client: Molto bene.
Guide: Here is your receipt. Thank you very much.
Client: It's nothing.
Guide: You're welcome.

Spanish Dialogue

Client: Buenos dias. Como esta usted?

Guide: Bien gracias, yo soy un guia para turistas y puedo llevarle a todos los memories Nacionales de la Capitolio, la Casa Blanca, Memorio a Lincoln, Jefferson, y el Cemetario de Arlington, la Tumba de Soldado Desconocido.

Client: Podremos ver tambien la Estatua de Iwo Jima?

Guide: Por supuesto que si . . . Vamonos . . . Sigamos ahora, tendremos tiempo hacer todo.

Client: Gracias amigo estamos listos hacerlo.

English Translation

Client: Good morning. How are you?

Guide: Well, thank you. I am a tour guide for the city tour. I can take you to all the national monuments of the capital city, the White House, the Lincoln Memorial, the Jefferson Memorial and Arlington Cemetery, to the Kennedy gravesite and the Tomb of the Unknown Soldier.

Client: Can we see the Iwo Jima statue as well?

Guide: Why, of course; let's go. If we leave now, we will have time to do it all.

Client: Thank you, my friends. We are ready to do it.

Chapter XX
The Presidency

Washington, D.C., is the great world city in our time, on which the fate and destiny of man depends. But the White House exercises the power to make major decisions that govern the world. Official business there at 1600 Pennsylvania Avenue, N.W., has made such an impact on the world that tourists will stand for hours in rain, heat, or snow to visit that famous house of the President. True, it is a most impressive house, situated on eighteen acres of land and containing 123 rooms, but in order to do the job he is sworn in to do, the president must have the aid of his Cabinet members. There is a division of presidential powers between the courts and Congress, and the many lobbyists in the city play a major part in influencing them. The president's strength lies in his advisers; Henry Kissinger, for example, as an adviser to Nixon was always on top of things—persistent and tireless in his quest to pull us out of Viet Nam. His routine of sacrifices and determination, even bordering on the brink of exhaustion, is notable; he felt the greatest source of strength in bringing about the meeting in the Rose Garden, where Richard Nixon was able to meet with the U.S. Marines and say, "We will bring peace; the peace that we will be able to achieve will be due to the fact that America, when it really counted, did not run away but stood fast, so that the enemy knew that he had no choice but to negotiate." Without Kissinger, Nixon could not have made those remarks.

Abraham Lincoln, the sixteenth president of the United

States, had no illusions about the presidency. He remarked in 1850, "Even to the most experienced politicians, it is no bed of roses. . . . No human being can fill that office and escape censure." Pres. John Adams, the first to occupy the White House, wrote: "The government of the United States is not in any sense founded upon the Christian religion." The presidents, from John Adams to George Bush, have failed to heed the repeated warnings of the Founding Fathers about the danger of mixing church and state, politics and piety. Colman McCarthy said in the *Washington Post*: "Religion is honored when it is separated from party platforms and valued for the moral force of faith and hope. It is dishonored when it is Americanized and militarized."* Earlier presidents have done one or the other. Reagan was the first to do both. The Holy Bible is the book that no one should be totally ignorant of, especially those who profess to take their direction from it. But to use the Bible in a way that the thought implied is a lie is to deceive oneself. We live in a time when military arms reduction talks have resulted in more arms; the analogy is "might makes right." Close observation shows that even our thirty-eighth president, from John Adams, is using the Bible to make Jesus a militaristic supporter of America's nuclear arms building.

In an article in the *Washington Post* (Saturday, February 16, 1985), Colman McCarthy points out that President Reagan said in a speech before the National Religious Broadcasters Conference in Washington, "You might be interested to know that the Scriptures are on our side in this." He then quoted Luke 14:31, "in which Jesus in talking to the disciples spoke about a king who might be contemplating going to war against another king with his 10,000 men, but he sits down and counsels how good he is going to do against the other fellow's 20,000, and then he says he may have to send a delegation to talk peace terms." At this piont, Commander in Chief Reagan became chaplain in chief: "I don't think the Lord that blessed this country as no other country

---

*© 1985, Washington Post Writers Group. Reprinted with permission.

has ever been blessed intends for us to some day negotiate because of our weakness." Reagan's flight into scriptural fancy was all that his fundamentalist audience could have hoped for. Many are from the Bible Belt and believe in the motto: If someone doesn't agree with you, get your Holy Bible and belt him with a quote. That's what Reagan was doing with Luke 14:31: You're a heretic if you won't turn the Prince of Peace into the Prince of War. Or as the bumper stickers on all those pickup trucks say, "God, Guns and Guts made America; Let's Keep All Three . . ."

The newspaper article went on to expose Reagan's ignorance of the Scripture; "Before the nation bows its head with Ronald Reagan and worships the Golden Nuke, a look at St. Luke's full text is in order. Reagan profaned the meaning of the parable. The next line after the king seeking peace terms because he had the smaller army is this: 'So, therefore, everyone one of you who does not renounce all that he possesses cannot be my disciple.' "

The text is about the cost of discipleship, in Dietrich Bonhoeffer's phrase. If one is going to follow Christ, it will cost plenty; if there is no renunciation of possessions, don't come. The point of the parable is not that a follower of Christ should get up a bigger army than the Pharisees-Soviets, but that a person should weigh his decisions before making them; by renouncing possessions, a person is free to place total trust in God. In the overall context of Christ's teaching and not Reagan's, the first thing Christ would renounce is weapons. The last people he would trust are politicians calling for greater militarism.

Being ecumenical in his religious dopiness, Reagan had an error for the Jews. He spoke of the relevance of religion in the modern world and "referred to the huge Menorah celebrating the Passover season in Lafayette Park" last December. Reporter Lou Cannon of the Post wrote that the Menorah is the ceremonial candelabra used during Hanukkah. Reagan's ignorance of Judaism is not new. In October 1983, he telephoned an official of the American-Israel Public Affairs Committee to thank him for supporting the administration's efforts to keep the marines in Lebanon: "You know I turn back to your ancient Prophets in the Old Testament, and the signs foretelling Armageddon, and I find myself wondering if we're the generation that's going to see that come about." Armageddon is not in the Old Testament, as Reagan, the Bible scholar, says. It is the last book of the New Testament, Revelations, by Saint John the Apostle.

Oh, well, what's the difference? Even a president can't be expected to get everything right. It's the idea that counts. But what is Reagan's idea in distorting religion for his own political ends? The Founding Fathers, seeking to protect pluralism, warned repeatedly against mixing church and state.

The Rev. Jerry Falwell, founder and president of the PTLA, has chosen a spiritually blind leader to solve the nuclear threat of the future. While Congress continues to cut off the top of the dandelion of racism, there is hope that the Black Caucus will put an end to the never-ending battle by dealing with the root. The first black neophytes of Congress saw the great need for the increased number of blacks that now make up the Congressional Black Caucus. The intricate functions of government today call for an enlightened, informed, and sophisticated member who has not lost touch with the faith of our fathers. Our team on Capitol Hill has come this far by faith, and to continue we must be proud of those who represent the power of our government. And the members of the Black Caucus must not forget that "We walk by faith not by sight" (II Corinthians 5:7). The young black recruits who will eventually replace the current power will get knowledge if their faith holds out. Let us remember the words of Martin Luther King, Jr. These words were stated by King himself long before he was assassinated. Since we live in two worlds, the Natural and the Spiritual, I will use the example of Martin Luther King's life and death to deal with the fundamental and humanist theories that confront us all, as far as our religious beliefs are concerned, as he spoke the following words in a sermon titled "Then My Living Will Not Be in Vain," delivered in February

1968. While musing, he said, "Every now and then I guess we all think realistically about that day when we will be victimized with what is life's final common denominator—*that something* we call death." And continuing on he said, "We all think about it, and I think about my own funeral. And I don't think about it in a morbid sense. And every now and then I ask myself what it is that I want said and I leave the word with you this morning."

He went on to expound, saying, "If any of you are around when I have to meet my day, I don't want a long funeral. And if you get someone to deliver the eulogy, tell them not to talk too long. And every now and then I wonder what I want him to say." Then in a deep muse he reflected, "Tell him not to mention that I have three or four hundred other awards—that's not important," and he added, "Tell him not to mention where I went to school.

"I'd like for somebody to mention that day that Martin Luther King, Jr., tried to give his life serving others. I'd like for somebody to say that Martin Luther King, Jr., tried to love somebody." And he went on to say, "I want you to say that I tried to be right on the war question. I want you to be able to say that day that I did try to feed the hungry. I want you to say that day I did try in my life to clothe those who were naked. I want you to say that day that I did try in my life to visit those who were in prison." And he said, "And I want you to say that I did try to love and serve humanity."

King was a student of human nature and affairs, like Milton, who was born a humanist, but the Puritan temper mastered him. John Milton was like a signpost on the journey through life of Matthew Arnold, who also embraced the fundamental theory of life after death. When Martin Luther King, Jr.'s day of destiny became imminent, he began laying claim on life beyond the grave, where dust corrupts. Martin Luther King, Jr., ended that sermon as he said, "Yes, if you want to say that I am a drum major, say that I was a drum major for peace. I was a drum major for righteousness. And all the other shallow things will not matter.

"I won't have the fine and luxurious things of life to leave behind. But I just want to leave a committed life behind."

He was finishing his message as though he had already had a premonition that soon these words which he was then speaking would be the same ones used as his own eulogy, and he continued by saying, "And that is all I have to say.

"If I can help somebody as I pass along,
If I can cheer somebody with a song,
If I can show somebody he's traveling wrong,
Then my living will not be in vain.

"If I can do my duty as a Christian ought,
If I can bring salvation to a world once wrought,
If I can spread the message as the Master taught,
Then my living shall not be in vain,"
he said in closing.
For here we have no continuing city but we
seek one to come.
—Hebrews 13:14.

And I saw a new heaven and a new earth, for the first heaven and the first earth were passed away, and there was no more sea. And I, John, saw the Holy City, New Jerusalem coming down from God out of heaven prepared as a bride adorned for her husband. And I heard a great voice out of the heavens saying, Behold the tabernacle of God is with men, and He will dwell with them, and they shall be His people, and God himself shall be with them. And He shall be their God. And God shall wipe away all tears from their eyes; and there shall be no more death, neither sorrow, nor crying, neither shall there be any more pain; for former things are passed away. And He that sat upon the throne said, Behold, I make all things new. And He said unto me, write, for these words are true and faithful. And He said unto me it is done, I am Alpha and

Omega, the beginning and the end. I will give unto him that is a thirst of the fountain of the water of life freely. He that overcometh shall inherit all things; and I will be his God and he shall be my son.
—Revelation 21:1–7

I cannot be put on probation;
You must believe every word that I say.
"Righteousness exalteth a nation;
Seek my face and continue to pray.
One must heed my admonition
And turn from your wicked way.
Then you will know vindication
And your night will be turned into day."

America is the invention of freedom,
America the home of the brave.
America the land of opportunity,
Was declared, for all but the slave.

If you're white, you're all right.
If you're brown, stick around.
If you're black, get back
And jump "Jim Crow."

"Jim Crow" was the name of a ministrel game originated in 1828,
By a man named Thomas Dartmouth Rice, whom many decided to imitate.
The popularity of Jim Crow went beyond the minstrel show,
And sentiment spread throughout the nation.
Thomas Rice, whose nickname was Daddy,
Became a glorified caddy,
Who mocked black people in his minstrel show and filled them with consternation.

The derogatory epithet Jim Crow became a designation, for
blacks, a feeling of woe
And a life of segregation.
In the heart of black American sequester.
The annoyance of the sore that festers
When criticized for the least aberration, renews blacks' claim for
liberation.

From the 1870s, Jim Crow legislation
Made laws demanding black and white separation.
The "separate" principle extended to school, parks and public
places,
And even cemeteries divided the races.

The higher power in the midst of the crisis of life
Is Jesus Christ, a man proven to be stoic.
When trusting in him average men become
Giants and begin to do exploits.

In the dramatic history of our country,
Men used words that are elastic,
Too many of our statesmen playing politics
Used them in rhetoric, merely bombastic.

Our history has shown people who wrote our Constitution
And from the abundance of their heart each one shared a part,
to perfect our search for absolution.

They are words of inspiration.
Spoken to inspire a fledgling nation.
When young America was yet within the cradle
Men came here seeking a life that was prenatal.
They came here from every shore;
And the vision of freedom that they bore
Had they remained where they were before would have been fatal.

Today we live in a time of politcal change,
In the midst of social revolution,
With race problems, drug abuse, sexual freedom,
And space travel added to the confusion.

Like the calendar, the clock, and the compass
We need an anchor in the strife.
Jesus said, "I will anchor thee,
I'm the way, the truth and the life.

"I'm the ship and the sea that you sail upon,
I'm the map to fathom the way.
I'm the sun that cast the shadow,
The creator of night and day."

My reasoning for making these statements stems from a summary of the results of the 1988 Democratic Convention as seen by the Rev. Jesse Jackson. He prescribed in a speech what he felt black Americans should do at this juncture in our quest for empowerment and justice, outlining the positive steps and gains of the campaign, pointing out the fact that hope was unleashed on the country and the faith of the desperate and disenfranchised whose spirits had been revived and had opened a way for sweeping changes in the composition and complexion of American politics. He made reference to the Rainbow Coalition as being alive and thriving as a result of the success of the 1988 Democratic Convention in Atlanta, Georgia, comparing political conventions to a quadrennial reckoning day and a time for us to measure our progress.

There were giant steps taken in Atlanta. The evidence of our impact on and the participation in that historic convention was unexpected. Jackson pointed out the fact that the full-scale integration of blacks into the convention was the culmination of three hundred years of struggles, not a fly-by-night phenomenon, adding that the great quest continues.

As Rev. Jesse Jackson continued to chart the course, he solicited the conventioneers to take a hard, long look at this watershed year to ensure that the gains made in Atlanta will have future meaning, saying we must continue our offensive against those who believe that government should be dedicated to the greedy and derisive of the needy. We must continue to press at the bounds of our political systems, demanding expansion of and inclusion in the decision-making process. No longer, he said, will we content ourselves with picking up voters, as people once picked cotton (referring to plantation days), and delivering them up to the "big house." We must assume our rightful places among those who make and influence policy.

Then Reverend Jackson said in a historic sense Atlanta '88 represents one round. In 1928, the first year in which blacks were allowed to participate in the Democratic National Convention (as alternates), they were barricaded behind a chicken wire fence on the convention floor. In 1932, the year that Franklin Delano Roosevelt first became the Democratic nominee for president, there were no black delegates. By 1948, there were but twenty.

In 1988, he said, 962 of the convention delegates, 23 percent of the total number of delegates, were black. The Mississippi delegation, which twenty-four years ago offered Fannie Lou Hamer and members of the Mississippi Freedom party two delegate seats as a compromise, this year was headed by a black man, Ed Cole, the state party chairman.

He went on to say, "We had unprecedented access to the Convention program." Of course, equally impressive was the number of officials nominated by our campaign, and he named those who had major roles in the program, including such speakers as Congressmen Charles Rangel of New York, Mickey Leland of Texas, and William Gray of Pennsylvania; Olga Mendez, state representative from New York; William Winpisinger, president of the International Association of Machinists and Aerospace Workers; Willie Brown, speaker of the California assembly; and

James Hightower, Texas commissioner of agriculture and the first white state official to endorse our campaign. And he said there was the heartwarming participation of the members of his family. About 20 percent of the Convention Committee members were black. Of those, 77 percent supported his campaign, Reverend Jackson said. In total, 79 percent of the black delegates were committed to his candidacy. So he asked, "What tangible effect did this heightened black presence have?" It meant that for the first time in the history of American politics blacks had substantial impact on the proceedings, including the drafting of the party platform, the philosophical reference book that will influence the dialogue of the fall campaign.

Reverend Jackson said we were able to get ten Jackson amendments inserted into the platform. Now, he said, they provide much of the doctrine of the Democratic party, such as focus on day care and prenatal care, declaring South Africa a terrorist state, and our program to wipe out illegal drugs.

We also carried, said he, from Atlanta several significant appointments to the Democratic National Committee (DNC). Other key DNC appointments included Mayor Sidney Bartholemy of New Orlèans, who is now vice chairman of voter registration; attorney Ron Brown, one of Jackson's aides; Rev. Willie Barrow, executive director of Operation Push; and Jesse Jackson, Jr., whose appointment was at the insistence of DNC chairman, Paul Kirks.

Reverend Jackson said involvement in Atlanta, therefore, was not tokenism and went on to say our representation in the convention hall was a reflection of our strength in the Democratic party. Blacks are about 30 percent of the Democratic vote. The 2 million votes added to the roles during his 1984 campaign, said Jackson, provided the margin that tipped the balance of the Senate back in favor of the Democrats in 1986 and defeated the nomination of Judge Robert Bork for the Supreme Court in 1987. People with as much stock in the corporation as blacks have in the

Democratic party must be treated as fully vested shareholders, the beginning of a new arrangement, a power sharing arrangement.

Rev. Jesse Jackson then made an unlikely analogy, saying, "Some people who were unable to see beneath the surface may have left Atlanta disillusioned. They said, 'We didn't get what we wanted.' I compare these people to the relative that you send to the grocery store with a pocket full of money to buy dinner. He returns empty-handed, claiming the store didn't have any steak. But you ask, 'What about the other meat, the vegetables and the breads? You don't come back with nothing because you can't buy steak?' "

Well, we might not have found steak in Atlanta, but we did not leave empty-handed, Reverend Jackson went on to expound, saying, "As a result of our campaign and alliances we formed, political seeds were planted that will bear fruit for generations.

"We have," he said, "established ourselves as the party of future." And he went on to explain that in the primary contest, we won the forty-five and under age group by a slim margin and handily won the eighteen-year-olds. He said more than 70 percent of our delegates were attending their first political convention and that these phenomena will have a significantly effective impact on the politics of the twenty-first century, adding that this group of up-and-coming policymakers has latched onto our message of hope and will force major changes in the political agenda.

Reverend Jackson said, furthermore, "Our campaign raised the ambition level of our leadership. We have broken through the psychological barrier that prevented blacks from reasonably seeking offices beyond traditionally black districts. Our expectations have skyrocketed. Now you have Louis Stokes of Ohio and Mickey Leland of Texas contemplating runs for the U.S. Senate and Mayor Andrew Young of Atlanta talking about running for governor of Georgia." Reverend Jackson added that we are just an attitude away from the White House.

an idea that many forces within the party are only now beginning to realize. So what you saw in Atlanta, Reverend Jackson was "But to get there," he said, "we must take some fundamental steps to secure our position. First we must vote on November 8. The press has focused on the presidential elections, but there is more than the presidency at stake. In excess of twenty thousand offices will be contested across the country on that day. We must be sophisticated enough to realize that our future depends upon our participation in these elections.

"We must see the power," said Jackson, "gained from the primaries and the Altanta Convention to demand reciprocal relationships with the politicians we have supported in the past." Then he said, "I won one hundred congressional districts in 1988 where I was not endorsed by the delegates or party officials. We must go back to those districts and either get a new understanding with those officials or get new officials. We need a commitment to integrate state making. That's politics at its root level."

And he said we must work to further our legislative agenda. State by state, we must pass same-day, on-site registration that is the key to empowerment. "We must also help to elect a president who is more committed to our agenda," Reverend Jackson added. "Michael Dukakis has pledged to support U.S. Rep. John Conyers' on-site, same-day voter registration bill, a piece of legislation thta would put millions on the voting roles and reduce the cost of our current registration process. Dukakis has made commitments to U.S. Rep. Ron Dellums' South African sanction bill and statehood for the District of Columbia, a measure that would add two U.S. senators and a governor to our ranks. He has also vowed to implement the economic set-aside registrations which would provide up to 50 billion in federal contracts to blacks and other minority businesses. Currently, because there is no apparatus to administer the economic set-aside bill, which, in effect, could be our forty acres and a mule, this vital resource goes untapped."

Jackson said, "While Dukakis represents public service, a commitment to affordable housing, a national health system and public education, George Bush and his boss, Ronald Reagan, have been a tool of private wealth." Jackson ended saying, "We must send George back to private life."

Then Reverend Jackson, compelled by the zeitgeist, said, "Our task is not easy. We must be disciplined and determined to achieve the total victory we seek. But we are too close to where we are going and too far from where we started from to be discouraged now. Much was accomplished this year.

"Not all of it was obvious, but then, how do you measure the significance of a changed mind? And through our campaign people's minds were changed, their expectations were changed, and emotional politics was changed. We took the moral high ground and brought together the distressed and downtrodden. Our growth has been substantial, and we are growing and winning each day."

The repercussions of segregation in the United States have gone beyond the periphery of only discriminating against the Afro-Americans in their quest for freedom here. The precepts of racist ideology find their way into foreign lands and countries, as in the experiences of Paul Robeson and Josephine Baker, who both (along with many others I could name) chose exile rather than deal with the people of their own land who have a penchant for raising lynch mobs against black people. At least until recently Europe was a favored place for the beleaguered Afro-American pilgrim to find refuge from the subtle and blatant racist tactics used here.

I have reached the conclusion, personally, that according to life's timetable, the night is far spent and we are approaching midnight. Nevertheless, we are still the last hired and the first fired. Black men make up 3.5 percent of the college population but 46 percent of the prison population; a black male's chance of being murdered before he is twenty-five years of age is one in twenty-three. Between 1976 and 1986, college enrollments for black male youths aged eighteen to twenty-four declined from 35 to 28 percent, and between 1973 and 1986 the percentage of black men eighteen to twenty-nine employed full-time year-round fell from 44 to 35 percent and average real earnings for black males fell by 50 percent; since 1970 the number of black households headed by women has more than doubled. If I were to continue with the statistics, you would see how the picture of black people in the United States in many ways has grown progressively worse. The spiraling death rate of blacks killing blacks is another form of genocide designed to kill off the frustrated black youth before he becomes aware of the importance of the terms of adhering to the democratic process and the aplomb of black people who have awakened and are storming the forts of the enemy. And the enemy comes in all colors, classes, and races. The principalities and powers, the spiritual wickedness in high places, are the enemies that all Americans must declare war upon. But in order to do so we must put on the whole armor of God. If we would become invincible in the face of nuclear war or whatever, we must not forsake the faith that this country began with in pursuit of freedom and justice for all.

Chapter XXI
What Does Jesse (Afro-America) Jackson Want?

By becoming the first black president of the United States of America, Jesse Jackson would put an end to the false belief that blacks are subhuman; this lie has persisted throughout history from the time the ten legendary blacks were brought to Lisbon and sold at the market. This not only represented the beginning of the slave trade in Africa, but also was the beginning of a strong delusion that plagued the early settlers to the New World up to this present time. It is still believed that blacks are inferior to whites even in the face of astounding evidence to the contrary. This belief is the root cause of Jesse Jackson not winning the Democratic nomination for the presidency in 1988.

History offers no parallel to the dramatic ascent of Negroes in the United States: no other country can match the ascent of a people who were slaves a mere hundred-plus years ago. Among the leading black achievers are: Marian Anderson, Paul Robeson, Dorothy Manor, William Grant Still, Duke Ellington, Ethel Waters, and Lena Horne in music; Katherine Dunham in dance; George Washington Carver, Percy Julian, Louis T. Wright, and Charles Drew in science and medicine; W. E. B. DuBois, William Stanley Braithwaite, and Charles S. Johnson in scholarship; Mordecai Johnson and Mary MacLeod Bethune in education; A. Phillip Randolph and Willard S. Townsend in labor; Gwendolyn Brooks (1950 Pulitzer Prize winner in poetry), Willard Motley, Langston Hughes, and Richard Wright in literature; Joe Louis and Jackie Robinson in sports; Edith Sampson and Ralph J.

Bunche (Nobel Peace Prize winners) in diplomacy. These are all pioneers in their various schools of learning for blacks who are an eternal reproach to white America. Their children have now dominated football, baseball, basketball, and track and field in sports. They have broken old records and are setting new ones wherever they go—in the Olympics, Pan Am Games, and national competitions around the world. They have integrated the Halls of Fame; they emulate their ancestors, who were disallowed by segregation laws to participate in past times.

The Black Menagerie

The black menagerie is America's shame
While the popular perpetration
Is that blacks are to blame,
But are we to blame when we try to relate
To the status quo prone to decide our fate?
Since the rape of Africa
When we were brought here in chains
The manacles are now gone,
But the bondage still remains.
Our liberated youth have abandoned
The black historic role,
But the majority through drugs and sex abuse
Have produced a hyperbole.

Opportunity has come knocking
At our economic door,
But drug addicts, drunks, and dropouts
Choose themselves to remain poor.
Too many have filled the prisons
And through peer pressure become slaves
While black martyrs and famous statemen
Must be spinning in their graves.

Nat Turner, Denmark Vesesy, Gabriel Prosser,
Men of valor,
Fought back against the slave system
Until death upon the gallows.
Giant Americans spoke out boldly against racism
Both black and white.
Shields Green and John Copeland died
With John Brown without a fight.

Their objective was to save black people
From the bondage they were in
And to free the souls of white folk
Who persisted in their sin.
Marcus Garvey, our great black hero,
Sought to set the captives free.
Uniting 6 million black folk
To exalt our pedigree.

He said, "Brother, hitch your hope to the stars.
Yes, rise as high as the stars themselves.
God has ordained you lords of His creation,"
Not to wallow in the mire like elves.
"Rise up; shake the pillars of the universe,"
Honorable Marcus Garvey would say,
"Seek solutions for all of our problems.
Remember this is our day.
Mighty men have gone before you
Holding forth their banners high
Men like Martin Luther King and Mickey Leland
Never feared to do or die."

In the face of opposition
We must rally to the cause,
Not like men with superstition
Who fear hypothetic loss.

"We walk by faith and not by sight,"
Apostle Paul declared,
So let's stand up and be counted,
For our victory must be shared.

There is a mighty black posterity
In America; take a look;
They excel in arts, sports, and music
While heading for the record books.
God has blessed us with the talent.
When we use it we are wise.
If we falter or procrastinate,
We'll end up with tear-filled eyes.

Wake up, Black America.
Break the shackles from your hands.
Your proud black ancestors
Have paid the price that you might stand.
Many have paid the supreme sacrifice,
Bodies molding in the grave,
But woe be unto us if we throw it all away.

Black people through toil and sweat
Have helped build this mighty nation.
The years of free and cheap labor
Have gone without due compensation.
Now if we feel we should be militant
Or that we must remain sore,
Then roll up our sleeves
And with a mighty heave
Beat that drug dealer from our door.

Drugs have caused us pain and sorrow,
And we all know that it's so.
We would have many more great black men
Had they only learned to say "NO."

There's a great big lying demon
Stalking the youth in our neighborhoods,
Saying, "Fast money is the only hope.
Go get it; damn the good.'
Then morals go out the window
And there goes the neighborhood.

We would all be a wiser people
If we would only stop and think.
God will make something out of nothing,
But drugs make monkeys out of men.
Fancy cars, gold chains, and diamonds
Are the trademarks of this brood
That pushes the poison to the next generation,
Destroying their chances to turn out good.
Party! Party! Party hearty
Is the byword of this clan
Then they point to our capitalist system
For a pretext to beat the man.

There are things in life more precious
Than the silver or gold,
Many things we take for granted.
It makes for the enoblement of the soul.
Let's not forget hard work is honest
And we've oftentimes been told
Man will profit nothing
If he gains the world and loses his soul.
If if comes to hell or high water,
Rich or poor, young or old,
We will accomplish little
If we never set a goal.

We are all prone to error
In this world of toil and strife,
But to stigmatize black people
While sin is rampant and inequity is rife
Is to deceive and delude each other
In the present scheme of things,
For what one sows he also reaps,
No matter what the future brings.

Traveling upon the sea of life
Without a predetermined destination
Is to wander aimlessly
Through circumstances and dire frustration.
One ship sails east, another west,
With the selfsame wind that blows,
But "it's the set of the sails
And not the gales
That determines the way we'll go."

Jesus Christ, our Lord and Savior, said,
"I'm the way, the truth, the life."
To all of us He is a calendar,
A compass and time device.

If we like ships are ever sailing
To an unknown distant port
Then like driftwood we'll remain afloat,
But we'll never reach the shore.
So why not seek Jesus for our direction
As we cross the sea of life?
He will serve us as a cloud by day
And a pillar of fire by night.

Time, distance, and direction
Must be observed for latitude.
The Word of God is sure protection
On the sea of life for longitude.
Christ has divided history
By his life and ill-timed death,
And if we choose to follow him,
We'll reach home, the haven of rest.

Jesus is our resurrected Lord,
He is Prophet, Priest, and King.
Though much derided,
Jesus makes believers and angels sing.
Whether we accept or reject him,
It matters not what men may say.
With him we'll face tomorrow
Being better off than today.

So we must learn to respect each other
Here now on this shoal of time.
But when we learn to love each other
Then he'll make our lives sublime.

It is not by happenstance
That America leads Western civilization,
For we're made up of every race,
Every strain and foreign nation.

No matter how loud or rowdy
The crowd caught up in bigotry,
Let's seek high hope in the sky
Like the apple pie.
God intended America to be free.

So, don't mock and call me Brother
Because I am black.
If you must call me Brother,
Lift the load from my back.
When you call me Brother,
Be sure that you're sincere.
For you remember that it was in chains
That I was first brought here.
I'm too related to debauchery and sin.
I'm much ostracized for the shape I was left in.
From the manacles of slavery
The process was slow
And my uphill climb
Was filled with penury and woe,
But if you judge me
Not by the color of my skin,
Then by all means call me Brother,
For I am America's true friend!

—Cecil Thompson, Sr.